Collected Poems and Translations

ROBERT WELLS was born in Oxford in 1947. He has worked as a woodman, a teacher, in publishing and as a freelance writer and translator. He is married, with two children, and lives in France. He is a Fellow of the Royal Society of Literature.

T0288222

ROBERT WELLS

Collected Poems and Translations

CARCANET

Acknowledgement

Grateful acknowledgement is made to *The Times Literary Supplement*, where three of the poems newly gathered here first appeared.

First published in Great Britain in 2009 by
Carcanet Press Limited
Alliance House
Cross Street
Manchester M2 7AQ

A CIP catalogue record for this book is available from the British Library
ISBN 978 1 84777 011 0

The publisher acknowledges financial assistance from Arts Council England

Supported by
ARTS COUNCIL
ENGLAND

Typeset, in Plantin Light, by XL Publishing Services, Tiverton
Printed and bound in England by SRP Ltd, Exeter

For Marie-Christine –
The book which should be yours, lost
In the life we share.

Contents

2

3   *Monte Gennaro Epigrams, One and Two*

4 *Sabine Portraits*

5

6

TRANSLATIONS

7 Virgil, *The Georgics*

8 Theocritus, *The Idylls*

NOTES AND INDEXES

Foreword

I have gathered my poems into six groups, each making a book within a book. The setting of the first is the coast of Exmoor; of the second, third and fourth, a stretch of hill-country in central Italy. The fifth belongs to the theme of erotic friendship and to one such friendship. The sixth is a miscellany in which poems on Persian themes and landscapes are followed by other poems of travel, and then by what is left, arranged as best I can. A seventh and an eighth section, containing translations of Virgil and Theocritus, have this in common with the rest, that the works concerned have been lived in, or lived with, as a place or person might be, my versions being a record of the experience.

1

The Winter's Task

The insects leave his toil. Frosts arrive
That starve the grass and bleach its paler growth.
Too thinly clothed amid the gathering cold
He works across the acres mute of change.
As the year falls back, he must yet persist
In the choice of effort, and outface till dusk
The weariness that forbids. The winter fields
About him spread their desert sympathy.

Standing by the white horse that nuzzles him
He touches the grey lips, to know what patience
Stables it out in light dark grass rain sun
And nothing kept, the stream run thin or full
That cloys and fumbles through the muddy field
And doles the pure fruit from its opened hand,
Presenting thirst, as air the breath, its gift
Derived in the same cold asperity.

For hand in hand with hope, life in his hands,
And clothed in powerful youth, he turns aside
From local ambition, even from the abyss
Of human feeling, though to stand at loss,
Frustrate or joyous amid the idle paths
Where nature cancels history, where strength
Of body is a means toward its own end;
And is the strongest he will ever be.

He lets his eyes fall on his folded arms,
Their yellow glint of hair, and tired his thought
Dwelling like sight heavily where it falls
And slow to move as he to lift his eyes.
He stirs at morning amid the ash of sleep
Light moving down an arm, moist shadow torn
Along the skin, the red, the white, the brown.
Dusk brings him ready to his food and sleep.

As each breath taken clears for strength a space
Of thirty seconds maybe to move free
And every movement hangs upon a breath,
He may think only of the next axe stroke.
Poor beggar of patience! The very thought
Reasoning his servitude discomfits it.
The end he labours for must seem the touch
Of sudden magic as he lifts his eyes.

His violence laid waste upon the hill,
His thirst extinguished in the lowly stream,
He conjures from a purified land at dusk
The hero's antique shrine; where at its hour
A bodily bright finished shape appears
And silent energies return, to offer
Their trophies rescued from inconsequence.
The cold increases. Darkness cheats the eyes

And he must come to himself, and long to break
The tryst of self-possession; setting his head
In the crook of his arm at night, and ignorant
What froze him at other times from company.
Then in the room his wakefulness becomes
A blank wall, shutting out the chosen scenes
Of memory, so that he lies in doubt
Whether the knowledge won begins or ends.

Imagined futures jerk his head from toil.
The bramble barbs that hook him back to lust,
And hope, a stray root withering in the air,
Melt nature's recalcitrance from his hands.
If the one constant is his own presence
Surely he labours toward his own defeat,
Creating only from the tempered land
A solitude askance amid the wild?

The stream set in its path, that runs more full
And gives suck to no trees; the chainsaw laid
Against the bark and drifting through the trunk,
Red and grey, chain black with oil, blue smoke;
Sycamore, blackthorn, willow mortified
To grey circles of ashes. When the task
Is finished, call it peace. Walls make a field.
Where saplings used to stand, the white stumps glare.

Daily his life wiped out, reduced each day
Toward this peace, the passive body sweet
And nature gentle in his mind, to live
By the blood's gradual renovating pulse –
It is not this youth is impatient for;
That labour so should neutralize its strength
Day upon day and year taken from year
Till darkness falls across a barren scree.

What part has patience here? What is content?
Less than a virtue; character broken down
Like leaves to soil, and as the spade turns up
The leaf's black imprint, so a man is found.
What end is the body? that he wakes remade
To quiet his heartbeat in a wider toil,
And all his being let go, that pulse through him
Leans toward the world still like a brimming depth.

His rest closes the day. When evening falls
All things attend upon his quietened sense
That keeps its watch, now self-possessed as they;
Distrusting sleep that comes without a name.
He wakes, as if such labour had not been,
Setting at break of day his hardened hands
And body's mastery to the one toil.
What can he keep from dusk but the one spoil?

The Stream

Inopportune desire! It runs to waste
Too cold for love, too bold for secrecy
And falls from fresh to salt, an altered taste
Where grassy covert gives to barren sea.

Bonfire

The fire burns deepest at dusk.
He watches lively flame
Possess the waste, dry sticks,
Green wood with its crisp bark
And terrified sap,

But all the same in a few minutes,
From green to black
To white ash and the shy ember
Falling clear of it, and his return
At daybreak fresh with sleep.

His Thirst

It was the utmost of his thirst
To set his mouth against the stream,
Leaning his hands on the wet rocks.
It was his nearest to content
To feel the inward cold slip down
And quiet his body with its touch.

Love's Default

This is my youth in love's default
To loiter on the verge of day.
I watch the bonfire flare and melt,
The disparateness burn away.

The fluent heat wave leaps and churns
And scattered sparks are caught within.
Brief quick vitality! It burns
Two instants if it touches skin.

The Colonist

1

He seeks a manner cleanly lean and spare,
Self-disenchanted, separate as the air,
Bodily silence poised amid his blood,
A virtue that no memory shall elude.
And peace is strengthless. How shall it abide?
Like rhododendron on a waste hillside,
Hydras of foliage burnished in the wind,
Memory persists, is rooted in his mind:
A soil made up of tiny filaments
Fed on itself, grown matted tough and dense
That throws a blanket over beds of stone,
Tree-stumps, and where the fallen trunks lie prone;
And broad leaves still from every vigorous stem
Unfolding in the spell of their own dream,
Glossy ungovernable and wildly kempt;
His virtue but a mask for self-contempt.

2

Lying down to sleep he thinks the body stilled,
Like broken armour on a battlefield
Thronged by the steady green and pocked with rain;
But wakes to rise and labours to regain
The peace withheld by vigour. All day long
He brings his strength to bear against the strong
Barrier of his own flesh while, lithe and thin,
Blood makes the veins stand bold along his skin.
Slowly the evening fills his silent stare,
Edging his forehead with cold foreign air,
And by the light that edge of cold lets shine
He sets the hero in the hillside shrine,
Transparent, near... How can the vision hold
Beyond his power to keep back the cold?
Starting, he shivers, and confronts appalled
A dusk that falls across the human world.

Emblem

A spring: the body kneeling to confess
Its mortal fault to water's blessedness.

The Hero

I clothe your body nearer than the dust,
Liven your weariness and taste your thirst.
I am the touch of air, a breath indrawn.
Number the attributes but I have gone.

'Life was not in your hands'

Life was not in your hands. You woke to it –
Like waters under earth amid your sleep,
A new divinity that had not yet
Possessed its virtues or its names to keep.

Effaced and by that presence so disowned,
Amid the unfenced land you stood aside,
Kept nothing but reserve. Where all your ground
Lay dispossessed, what ground had you for pride?

If the land were less derelict, you might say
You tamed the solitude through which you move,
But you clear paths to lead yourself astray
And endless wilderness their windings prove.

The tiny space you make into a field
Between two hillsides and a wall of sea
Surrounds you emptily amid the wild.
It is the part of you that is not free.

The Will

The Will is an empty house.
You are free to enter.

It is the unlighted room,
The undusted floor.

Nothing awaits you there
But your own presence

And the petty tasks by which
You serve yourself.

A Caution

Look at the land with love, but don't confuse
With your own flesh the field, the path, the hill.

When pressed to serve more than a human use,
Their blankness mocks the effort of your will.

New Year

The cleared hillside paler in the winter's day,
The fire melting now, single, a sobered glare:

The tangle and dead-weight are lifted away;
Stray song of birds ornaments the leafless air.

The Young Woodman

He knelt, placing his hands
On the stones beside the stream
And bent his face to the water

For the lips
That would not shape themselves to his.

★

'When I looked for myself
I found trees, paths, water, sky, hills.
I found everything that I saw and touched.

These filled me –
There was nothing left of myself.'

★

His nature was mild like the fields.
It was the soft turf under his tread,
The alteration of weather.

But desire was in his nature too
And that was not like the fields.

★

The elements were hands
That had stripped his body
And went over it, he stood still –

And they felt it as if they were fashioning it
So that no other love could be made.

Woodman's Song

Heather, bracken, whortleberry fail.
My solitude is like this patch
Of stones, set randomly together
Against the encroachment of gentle grass,
    And without use or change.

Dew knits its web across the turf,
Deepens the colour of rotting leaves
By the path, eases the earth to mud.
No colour deepens across the stones,
    No weather blunts their edge.

Mightn't my solitude be the pool
Where at dusk deer come to drink,
Slotting the border with their hooves;
From where the stag's uncomforted bellow
    Carries when night has fallen?

Mightn't my solitude be these larch trees,
Leaning, derelict, on one another?
Mightn't it be the windtorn ash
That spreads above a grove of seedlings
    And its own tumbled limbs?

Mightn't the presence of these things,
Dewy, intensifying to a glitter,
Image the humanness of my body?
Couldn't I keep this light within me,
    Precarious and unspilled?

Heather, bracken, whortleberry fail.
My solitude is like this patch
Of stones, set randomly together
Against the encroachment of gentle grass,
    And without use or change.

On the Hillside

I could not speak to him, but what we shared
Was the water drunk in the interval of toil,
The stream running over our wrists,
And I shared some biscuits with him that I had.
The water washed the crumbs about our mouths.

I could not speak to him. He was afraid of my glance
And jerked away from it to work harder
At throwing what I cut on the fire.
I was glad of his presence there on the hillside
Where the loneliness was mine and not to be shared.

★

Through unmellowed stones
The stream finds its way.

It was here he drank
Here I watched him lean,

Hands on the wet rocks
Face to the water –

Standing then, thirst quenched
And wiping his mouth.

On the Doorstep

The blush that floats amid the new-cut grain
Of ashwood is the same as in this sky.
    I greet the morning

But with the child's half-asleep affection
Who, sitting up, bemusedly receives
    The embrace that wakes him.

The Axehandle

Calling my eyes back from the sea
– With adoration I watched the horizon lift
Above the headland, far up against the sky –
And looking instead for a human token
Even at this distance, to hold me back,

I noticed the axe where I had put it aside
– How the balanced ashwood handle
Was like a limb with its muscle shaped to use,
An arm graceful and certain with hillside labour
Evidencing the generations of hands.

At the Pathside

The touch of air that greets you as you walk home
Flickering across the surface of your thirst –
It is the last grace to be won
Before dusk takes the world.
Blood brims your body to its furthest bound.
Your senses fill what you see.

Do not outstay the blood's heat.
The landscape that is now so close
Will drain from your perception,
And day will leave you at the pathside,
Cherishing foxglove leaves, or shaping
A crown of moss for a face not to be found.

After Haymaking

The last bale placed, he stretched out in the hay.
    Its warmth and his were one.
He watched the fields beneath the weakening day
And felt his skin still burning with the sun.

When it was dusk, he moved. Between his skin
    And clothes the sweat ran cold.
He trembled as he felt the air begin
To touch and touch for what it could not hold.

Haymakers at Dusk

From the top of the stack I could see,
Through the open-ended barn,
The light going out of day
As the heat of effort had gone.

I heard them talking beneath
As they stood about at ease.
The words fell through their breath
Like stones, and into space.

Haymaker

Work is finished. He stands in the dark field,
Cleared of its bales, the last trailer gone in.

A delusive freshness reaches through his body
As if moonrise were the sign for him to begin.

At the Back of his Mind

It was like a wall, or a tall earthen bank
With flames beginning to streak the green and brown.
At night in the city amid the hectic bodies
Which followed the music and were followed by eyes,
He would discover it at the back of his mind.

He had forgotten the solitude, the touch
Of air on skin, water in the thirsty mouth.
This was the memory that remained with him,
Grass, earth, branches and flame melting together,
Of the steep hillside where he had laboured once.

Impasse

The attempt of youth
To vivify the inanimate –

Once it has been made,
The man will never tire

Of recalling, detail
By detail, the impasse

In which he would choose
To find himself again.

The Day

1

I stand on the doorstep. The land is shadowy,
The sky a red-faint veil – it hardly lights the earth
But is more splendid, more visible than at noon.

They must be wished, the twilit cold and the blank hours.
I gather up chainsaw, fuel, billhook, a small axe
And turn down from the path across the steep hillside.

2

Here the impenetrable wall of fallen trunks,
Saplings, the knit undergrowth of rhododendron
Begins, which day by day I cut back foot by foot.

I rekindle the fire, start the saw, and slowly
My sluggishness changes to a warm ebullience
Which fills my chest as I breathe, and moves in my limbs.

3

Engaged, I give myself to what I see and touch.
This beech coppice, these unmellowing stones, this soil
Are inward events, appearances of a dream

Which matches in everything the world outside me.
To reach that world, to break from the mute trapped turmoil
Of body to an unhindered apprehension!

4

The shrill of the saw, the crash of green, the flaring
Heat of flames surround me, my skin liquid with sweat.
My strength is the obstacle I must break beyond

To attain the clear extreme of water or fire.
I pause, look out unreadily at distant coombs
And the wide Channel; then go more fiercely to work.

5

What I labour to resolve is there as before,
Will not be altered. But moments interrupt me
When, gazing at the broad expanse of land and sea

Bleached into pale colours beneath the winter sun,
My existence ceases to be mine, and becomes
The existence of all things my senses light on.

6

Hunger gains on this unselfed rapture. I break off,
Climb back to eat. What then of the contradiction
Between crass appetite and purged extremity,

The spirit and the human fault? When I return
The trance persists. Like the day it is at its height,
Then like the day it begins to change, to deepen.

7

The moments of effacement become intervals
In which I stand and gaze wherever my eyes fall.
The sea loses its lively brightness, the shadows

That stretched from crannies and branches, interlacing
The afternoon sunlight, fade to make one shadow.
Labour and its relief meet and are of a kind.

8

Dusk. Re-entering my fantasy of struggle
I pile the fire with cut sections of fallen trees,
Wrestle the trunks of rhododendron to the ground.

Earth is already crisping with frost. I touch it
And lift my hand, startled, from the brittle softness.
A dark blue sky, illuminated by the moon.

9

My body has moved every way, is competent
In all its muscles. The impulse of affection?
Giving no sign, it rises still and disperses.

Unbrokenly visible, the loved horizon
Accounted for me. But to be found past nightfall
Staring out at a landscape that cannot be seen…

10

The enchantment vanished, I come back to myself.
Am I the possessor of this flesh, this heartbeat?
Identity has dwindled to a tiny thread

Running through a rough-skinned hand. I gather my tools
And climb back from the hillside to the level path
(Strange to my feet the sudden ease of walking there.)

11

I trim and light a lamp, sit over some strong tea,
Lay the fire, light it, wash and eat. Then the evening
Is mine, a clear space in which I can be at rest.

I sit by the fire, unmoving, without feeling.
My senses recompose the landscape and the day –
The horizon bounds me; I lose my body's line.

12

Rested, there is a restiveness that coexists
With this ease and vision. It invades the blank limbs,
A dank stifled undergrowth unreached by the sun.

What expectation has been trapped, what hope disowned?
It is a longing in disguise to be set free,
By shared affection, from this elemental care.

Morning

Like mist from water
Sleep steals from the body

Which is discovered
Anew, standing on earth,

The hours before it
As red pales from the sky.

At Dusk

I tremble at the edge of strength, aware
        What panic lies beyond.
My warmth disperses in the frosty air.
I touch the brittle softness of the ground.

Gathering my tools, some kindling for the hearth,
        I leave the unfinished task
And climb the hillside to the level path,
Its red earth almost colourless in the dusk.

Meridian

With a glance I sent myself out to the furthest edge.
The sea, whispering, was my bloodstream.
                                    All there, all one,
A glitter, a certainty, land and sea extended –
Body of the world, to which my senses were given.

Vesperal

It falters in the cold air,
Disperses with the heat of labour;

It has gone, my separate joy,
And cannot be reclaimed

By the effort of memory
Nor shared with another

– A body laid warm
Against the freezing dusk.

A Fantasy

A fantasy of battle:
With fire and steel I fight across the ground.
Unfalteringly the sun withdraws. I struggle,
        Running against the bound

Of warmth and strength, to cram
My fury from the last reserve within.
The moon's cold challenge finds me. Here I am,
        Clear, ready to begin.

Larchtrees

Sun catches the larchtrees
First thing in the morning,
Colouring their trunks
As if with the warmth of rested limbs.

I can hear the owls from them
Last thing at night,
Sending out long calls
Muffled like the beams of light in fog.

'A patch of grass'

A patch of grass on scree.
How could it have taken root there?
I lift the stone aside –

Crusting the surface
A pinch of soil, light and dry,
Which wind blows from my fingers.

'The fogbound dusk'

The fogbound dusk thickens to rain.
I notice amid the gorse verge

A glow-worm's green shine,
And stoop there, fingering the grass aside.

A Stag at Sea

(forced out by the hounds)

Head back in the crisp waves and antlers back,
The winter mane sea-darkened at its neck,
A fated creature, never out of view,
Treads water in the empty field of blue.

The Fawn

Starting, clumsy and graceful,
From the clumps of bracken at my feet

A fawn tumbles downhill –
Then gathers itself away into the thicket.

'At the head of the coomb'

At the head of the coomb
I startle a young hind.

Wide eared and eyed,
She stands at gaze an instant.

Then the resilient sinew
Of her walk breaks to a gallop –

'O lovely creature…'
And I run to keep her in view.

Poaching on Exmoor

In the instant of the shot
The stag raised its head
So that the bullet passed too low,
Through the neck;
And cramming all its anger
Into this moment of offence
It turned and charged at random,
Not marking what had broken the silence
Or brought this sudden pain
From the gentle woodland.

But at once anger dwindled
To an instinct for escape
So that after a few bounds
It veered off into the thicket.
Its legs had not yet learnt
That all its strength was gone,
That the quick circuit
Of its life was broken;
Till in mid-bound
They lost themselves, failed to lift.

It lay filling the coppice
With the rank smell of its maleness,
Brown mane thick at the neck,
Legs tapering and darkening
To black hooves.
   Stepping from the trees
They came to get it with ropes,
And searched the ground but in vain
For a missing antler
Broken off in the flight.

Clearing Ground

The hawthorns grew crowded together
In what had been the hill-field.
I had to cut whole thickets away,
Trunk by trunk, before they would fall.

The trees were just in bloom.
I looked up through their dead-seeming
Mesh of twigs at delicate green,
White flowers, open sky –

O need to make things simple by levelling them!

★

I threw the trees, cut into fragments,
On the fire, and watched the green crumple
In an instant in the flame.
                    Later I would find
A twig with flower and leaf still intact
By the circle of the ash.

★

My harshness was the saw's
As it cut through the thicket wall;
My pleasure was the neat blankness
Of cleared ground.
                    Looking across
The shallow curve revealed
Where two slopes met
I would think, 'It was impassable; now
To cross it is as simple as drawing breath.'

I would lie down there,
Spread out my arms and watch the sky.

Bonfire

The heaviness of the waste –
Barely to be lifted, a bramble bush on a fork.

Bracken, tons of it, broken down
Year upon year;
          and trees
So delicate, tapering in the air,
Bulky and gross once fallen.

★

Fire crystallizes about evergreen stems.

On hawthorn bushes the tips of thorns
Ignite and glow.

          A mesh of birch twigs
Turns black together, some dark smoke
Playing slowly above them amid the flame.

★

What is the fire?
          It flares or fades
By its own unaccountable law.
There will be the slightest gust of wind
And at this sign it takes,
Making no barrier of
Branches, foliage,
The heaped tangle of thorn
Through which it mounts, pouring upward.

I watch the materials caught
In the rush of heat,
How leaves, stems, twigs
Lose heart, crumble about themselves,
Fold in,
As if the first impulse
Were to withdraw and so escape;

25

And then, in the very process,
Fly weightlessly apart, upward,
Glowing and crisping,
Turning black, then white, then gone.

*

Masterly strength:
                    There was a moment,
Once ash and burning charcoal had been amassed
Sufficiently, past which the fire
Would take anything,
Break it of its nature,
Melt it towards itself
– A shape become indistinguishable
In the soft white-red circle.

Six Emblems

1

From the felled trunk the bark
Has rotted away, its wood
Worn into a fibred relief;

Grey-white the scars where branches
Splintered, shrunken the bracken
Which covered it in spring;

Years since the severed life
Died out. What life it has now
Is from the winter sun.

2

The sea's blue at dusk, tiled with waves,
Glazed by the mist,
Deepens.

Across it from the steep-edged coomb
A beech-trunk lifts,
Pale in the drying wind.

3

Sun opening the coomb
In the morning
Moves down the side and curves out anew
The gentle incline of its lap,

Like a human goodwill
Illuminating the mind
That dwelt winterlong in shade
As though the shade were life,

And reaches
With a sense of warm discovery
Over budded trees,
Bent bracken, brittle leaf.

4

The sapwood rots;
But where they lie embedded

The hard little cores of broken twigs
Stay sharp.

5

Day overcast:
A patch of intenser brightness

Folds itself away amid the atmosphere,
Shedding light on the sea –

★

Clarity that, unable to attain
Full sway,

(Some flaw of will preventing it,
Some loss of heart)

Withdraws, prefers to fade,
Leaving only its shadow in the mind.

6

Spermatozoa of flame
Seed the dark, curling
Long momentary tails.

The fire flares at ease –
Could not burn harder
Or be more sheerly itself.

A Motto

My eyes to the land
My skin to the air

My thirst to water
My memory to fire

After the Fire

Stunting shade,
The leaning back towards light;

The wind's shape in the coomb, bending
The tops of larches over, so that they lie
Along the bank of its current
Like sand at a stream's edge;

A hard winter, a burgeoning summer,
A storm, a snowfall –
The evidence in cut wood-rings, torn-off boughs;

A sycamore trunk stripped of its bark by squirrels,
The shredded patch
Where a stag rubbed its itching antlers in spring;

A main-shoot bitten short;

Also like sand the fluted pattern,
Graceful and smooth,
Where for years one branch has blown against another:

Small disparatenesses, the thousand accidents,
All gone to ash.

Making a Bonfire

At first I cut carefully what I put on the fire
And lay it carefully,
Twigs, leaves, only a log or two,
So that it won't burn hollow;
Then as heat starts to hold
And the fire is more than a burst of flame –
Has accumulated and springs
From a core of burning ash –

No need to cut up much what I throw on;
It will take branches whole.
The lively flame reaches and plays
Long about the bent and straight, feeling
Through the tangle with its subtle touch
And roaring when it takes.

★

So when the senses
Are kindled, I think, feed them with self –
Slowly at first,
Twigs, leaves, logs,
Cut small, laid carefully;
Then, when flames reach
(What is the flame?)
From the burning fall of ash
(What is the ash?)
Throw on whole branches, dragging them downhill,
One on another, those you need to be rid of,
To clear the ground
For planting, or so that you can walk easily
At least –
Let the flame take them
And melt them unaccountably
In its own way.
Don't let the fire burn hollow,
The branches subdue the flame,
Seared so that they blacken the hands
And the hands the face –
A smoking crisscross of sapwood;
And no enlivening blaze
Hurries you to work, to find more
Before what is there is consumed.

★

The ash sifts and settles,
The fire burns down
In a circle.
                    What is left at the sides –
Pull it away, cut by the flare's extent,
Dried now, quick to draw the flame;
Throw it on; and again
Till nothing is left:

A white-red circle
Bold to the eye when dark falls
Across the cleared hillside.

'When days open'

When days open and air softens
And sun spills over the sides of hills
That had lain in shade,

Shall body and heart resist?
What else was winter
But a grindstone against which they were set?

Sparks rushed, brittle and heatless,
Against unfeeling hands.
The axe was lifted away, made sharply bright.

Now the birds' undertone
In the morning,
Delighted, sensual, pure –

What is this but the body's ease,
Waking satisfied
And grateful for its dream?

The Forester

Five for S.A.

1   *A Felling*

For hard hat, you wore a knitted green cap
To keep woodchips and oil out of your hair.

Poised on its wooden hinge, the enormous beech
Seemed to leap from its base, swung ruinously
Through the air;
                a slow shock, a long crash –
Branches shattering under their own weight
As the wide canopy folded in on itself,
Continuing to collapse while the trunk lay jammed
Against the gouged-up rubble of the coomb-side.

A shallow root tearing up from where you stood,
You toppled back lightly, chainsaw in hand
– Its blade as long, almost, as you were tall.

2   *A Morning Shot*

Your rifle club, 'The Outcasts'! Week by week
A score in the high nineties might be remarked
In the sports-page's small print. Your other tally
Went unrecorded.
                Poacher turned gamekeeper
(On either side, equally clandestine),
You had your cover – a contract forester
Labouring in odd corners – to justify
Your out-of-the-way appearances and errands,
And kept odd hours, the same hours as the deer.

In your outcasts' realm a strict morality
Prevailed. Joke and mischief were its medium,
A picaresque justice the staple of your talk:
How you had the goose off the front lawn of the man
Who paid you short; how, on the day your rivals,
The Hunt, came down, the carcase of a stag

Lay under logs in the back of your parked truck.
– Against its side, binoculars in hand,
Leant some hunt-followers, scanning the long coombs
For the vanished quarry.
                              You had been up early –
Your quiet catchphrase, 'I'll just have a look around.'

3 *Below the Moor*

Coombs of wrecked oakwood, rhododendron, scree;
An estate's slow overwhelming of itself:

Who would not have been discouraged or have connived
At the settled dereliction?
                              But your energy
Came easily, naturally, as if its source
Lay beyond you in some larger principle
Of activity, drawn on at need by you: a small man,
Only so much of body as might serve
To be the principle's agent.
                              Then no inertia.
The land, as you looked out on it, was tense
With unsprung incident, the deer lying up
On inaccessible slopes. A quickening knowledge
Joined you to what surrounded you, vast views
Of near and far, spacious and intricate;
A field of adventure in which you moved
Secret and cautious, or running like a boy;
Calculating as far as you could, then reckless,
Agilely daring…
                              It was the release of event
Which pleased you, always the participant
Whether as perpetrator or as witness;
Least mere onlooker when most you seemed so.

4 *Lumber*

Three beechtrunks, trimmed and blunt, awkwardly lying
Aslant the slope, ready to be winched down;
You in a tractor on the drive below:

The noosed cable tightened and jerked, dragging
The first, imprisoned in its own deadweight,
Some heavy yards.
                                    Suddenly, freakishly,
It rolled, lifted, slid over the smooth bark
Of the trunk beyond it, and jumping lithely clear
Struck the third a huge dull knock broadside.
Then, with lunging slippery momentum,
Skittish almost, as the ground dropped away,
All three together hurtled towards the drive.

From the open cabin came a whoop – long-drawn,
Rising, more shout than cry, more song than shout;
It was your welcome of the incalculable
As the trees bore down.
                                    They fell in a harmless fork
Around the tractor, to be hauled then to the side
(After a pause of cheerful astonishment),
Laggard, neutralized, to await collection.

5 *In Hiding*

To accompany the presence and happening
Of things, the light and weather in their changes;
Disqualified by no deranging action,
To make of myself mere consciousness of things
– So to live only in their living through me
And with their entirety to become entire
Was what I aimed at.
                                    Whether the need to hide
Came first, or sprang from this, I never asked.

If clandestinity gave the common ground
On which we met, yours was of another kind,
Practical, outward. You hid to intervene,
As hungry for the event as I fought shy of it;
Your shot irretrievable, its report and echo
Filling the coomb, splitting the morning's calm,
Dividing before and after by a wound, a death –
The evident trespass you would get away with.

Ashton

Trees were suddenly leafless.
Slates on the farmhouse roof
Lay brittler, colder, duller.
Dusted with grit and green
The outhouse sagged more bare
– Frayed boards, putty scaled-off
About each loosening pane.

The heath raised itself up
Darkly beneath a closer
Sky. Sheep coughed in the pen,
Starting to the dash
Of the dog, like grass to wind.
The dog would whimper and cower
For a touch, word or look

To brook a weather
That pried the weakness of trees
– Eponymous grove of ash,
Sentinel beech; and livened
Only the native damps
Of the house, built as it was
Across a hidden stream.

A Memory of Exmoor

On Sundays, walking between the sea and moor
Through derelict woods, up to the dry-stone wall
    That crowned the Sugarloaf,

I'd linger by a gate among hawthorn trees
Encrusted to a grey coral of lichen,
    Where a lost path turned off,

And imagine it the setting for some 'tryst',
The word unreal enough not to beg questions,
    Let alone challenge me

With the clear response cutting through fears and hopes,
That might have come (had someone really been there)
    To test the revery.

Before Sleep

Though I fall back
The day has been completed,
Dawn to dusk
Filled with labour to the edges.

Though I fall back
The writing is on the page,
Still holding
The world that has slipped from my hands.

2

Further on Down

The vine leaves cup their copper sulphate spray.
The dark plums loosen here. A swallowtail
Crawls by a hornet and a flat
Beetle varnished like a green toenail.
But hill should come over hill, bay over bay,
And the mist hide what we be the first to chart –

Here the only goodness is the sweat
Falling forward as the body leans to the pick.
Closer than a snake in its slippery skin
Senses the earth I want the feel of earth,
And hour after hour as if to exhaust the rock
The shaft jars at the blows I lie beneath.

The pick starts with sparks. I lift it, want to go
Further on down as if each blow
Suddenly might find out for me the ease
Of the mind's movement, and release
This force so that it lets the body go –
Further on down, as if to exhaust the rock.

'Sure in its strength'

Sure in its strength the body drew
Stones with deliberateness to the chest,
With accuracy spaded the earth into
The panniers slung over the mule.
                                    There was
Surely a mood of real content
When dusk unfocussed the air's smoky glass
And made the olives plumes of a grey mist
And my skin was grey with sacks of cement

Cattlemen

Dry sticks laid across
A piece of paper stained with oil
And a fire where we halt.
The sweat falls off and we drink
A mouthful of water and feel the cold.

The mule suddenly seems a lighter colour.
In the half dark
The fire paints strokes over the long muzzle
And flat hard forehead
And the forelegs

And the men move
Like more than men possessed
By their own lives,
Become what is evidenced by the rounded stones
Close in the path

And the rough stones lying like scree
At the side.
There are meetings here and things said
Though full light brings
Them back to themselves.

Breakfast

The pasture is a faded white.
Even the food palls
At the mountain's height by the spring,
A loaf in halves, unwrapped
From a blue cloth.
                        Oil and salt,
Raw ham. Sitting apart
To let the horses drink unscared
They brood what dream was broken
When mother or wife
Called them at four.

Shape of Air

It has lighted on you, this shape of air.
I don't want you to know that it is there:
Not yours or mine, as by the gate you stand
That divides the mountain from the worked land
And the first light of day, neither shade nor shine,
Shows through your open shirt your body's line.
The stones, the coppice, the inconsequent trees,
The cold fountain by the path, where blackberries
Rot on the bushes unpicked, and before noon
The cattlemen, work finished, will rest from the sun:
How casually you come here, bring that shape,
Stretch in the grass, drink from the metal cup
Its cramping mouthful; certainly of this place,
Your muscle-rumoured limbs and quiet face,
Your cheerfulness. O beat the earth at a joke
With open palm, it was the same smile broke
An age ago here, and the same shape lit.
The same hope as mine was effaced by it.

Vendemmia

And your dialect blurred with locality, I think,
As the grapes with mist. We work along the rows
Stripping the bunches from the vines, while I puzzle
For sense in this tender meaningless conceit.

Asleep

A sheet of cardboard from a packing case
Spread on the concrete floor: with knees drawn up,
Hands wedged between, he sleeps; his life drawn back
Within itself from the sealed eyes, the face.

Contadino

He goes under the deep-coloured shelter
Where moss and bramble overhang the road
Hid in the muted colour of his clothes,
And when the rain has stopped, appears again
Steadying the crooked beam cut for a plough
That weighs his shoulder, and continues down.

Bedding sometimes in the corrugated shack
That he exchanges in summer for his home,
The weather flocked about his sense, he knows
What is happening and watches before sleep
Awake to the quick air, the loosening rain.
Rust from the roof shakes down into his eyes.

He takes his backwardness from the slaked land,
His limbs from tree roots bleeding to the spade,
His body in the dulled confusion of sleep
From loamy soil. But suddenly visible
It will break cover before day and move
Against the twilight, free of its own ground.

The Mill

If any man should come to clear the mill
That stands here derelict and hides the stream
He will discover, hidden and still there,
This dank recess, a tunnel flanged with lime
Where the millstream exclaims, and idly falls
Across the rock and bearded stillicide;

And looking up, will see where the current sprang
At evening when they shut the millwheel off
And might imagine how, compelled more fine,
When day began it burst against the blades,
But what most draws him in a secret shared
Is where the water shoots its whitening plume.

So he will stand and finally go back.
When he emerges from this powerful place
That limestone girdles round with yellow bowel
He will begin to work as if his hands,
Lopping the willow and unclothing walls,
Stripped from the body what is not itself.

The Bathing Place

He turns feeling the straw through the blanket
And turns from himself and rises and a dream
Possesses him for darkness and the air.
Then walking flowers from his hollow sleep.
His feet must lead him to the hollow where
A gravel pool is channelled from the stream

To make a bathing place and he must dive
And turn again when he comes up and watch
The mottling of the moon upon the surface
Gather in flashes to the body's white
That thirsts beyond the feel of its own grace
Toward the unbalancing dark, the water's touch.

But air and water, dark and light compose
A melting altar and a blade let fall.
He must take back his gift and stand aside
And fully waken, shivering. As he dries
The moon outstares him, the sealed hills preside
Like elders who withhold their ritual.

Afield

As neat and separate almost as the body
That labours there, the field. Compare them then,
But say the labour has no end, and say
It tasks him to the limit of his strength.

The Attributes

1

Here are the path, the field. He takes this way
Setting his footprints in the spidery dew
Hunched from the rain, a sack about his shoulders
Lost as he moves, the sun's automaton.

Only the attributes can be expressed,
The body's useless grace, its constancy
Where impulse has no strength and these enough
To bear the sense of his surrendered soul.

2

His clothing mutes his skin as fate his soul
Gathering sweat and dust. Body and land
Touch on its reticence and are withheld,
Join there in secrecy and are absorbed,

So that he stays both weathered and unformed
And like these stones that go to make the walls,
Grizzled and worn but if you turn them over
Still white and even, still of the riverbed.

3

He watches daylight empty from the fields
That run to waste beyond the worked confines.
Their strengthless fancy was his thoughts' reserve
Softening each gesture with a fallow grace.

His disaffection is the wind that thickens
Amid the hazel scrub on his path home
Unfed, unwashed, the latest passer there
Whispering that body is the commonest thing.

4

Weakness commands. His strength is servitude,
Limbs that are matched against the endless clay,
Reproach that loiters where the brown back strains
And nothing sweetens, nothing is brought to him.

Diving into the cold, his startled blood
Shrinks and dilates again and rediscovers
A sobered joy, or crouching toward the stream
He starts to wash and then forgets to move.

'O wilful spirit'

O wilful spirit whose thin hands surprise
The crayfish of its hueless independence
And pelt the viper in its sulky creek
And murder the huge toad in its dank roost,

Poaching upstream along the banks and pools –
My dream is the pretext of your sacred lust.
God of the fields, more haunting than presiding,
As vengefully as life persists, you live.

A Dream

He wakes in the last instant of a dream
And feels its diminishing explosions
That shake his sleep across the sudden distance
Like bridges blown, securing a retreat.

Off the Path

The pool was hindered
By briars but when he broke through
He found the sides were clear except for moss
And the smooth straight stems of a figtree.
It was a stroke more than the length of a body,
Pale with shadow,
Deep as a body, and at one end the stream
Came flustering down a roughened fall.
Pebble and briar and leaf
Had fastened into reefs of lime.

He stood on the green brink,
Took off his boots,
Listening and looking at the barrier of thorns
That screened him from the path.
His hesitance was of the world. It screened
A life he could not guess.

But he had a white inkling of it
As he bent and let himself in,
Not thinking of the cold;
And standing on the floor,
The limy sand pleasant beneath his feet,
He watched the water waving
His body like a crumpled flag.

He put his head under, then swam a stroke
And laid first his forehead
Against the bed of the waterfall
Then his whole body, leg chin and chest,
And stretched out his arms.
He felt the water against his cheek,
Its noise filling his ears,
Then put his head under again, right down
Till it knocked against stone at the bottom
And ached with cold.

He dressed quickly and could not remember
The moment that he stood naked
When he had emerged,
His feet smaller in his boots and his clothes
Pulled hastily over wet skin. He started
To run and went on running
Into the twilight,
Joining its silence to his speed.

Deus Loci

Imagine the embodiment of what drew you here,
A God standing on this mossed outcrop of rock.

He is on the edge of appearing, and is withheld
Only by so slight a thing as his absence.

The Unnamed Pool

'Why have you left the path? What makes you stare?'

'This water, pale beneath the darkening air,
Haunts with a look that I must try to forget
Or to meet fully.'

                    'Its look cannot be met.
There is nothing to meet there, neither a challenge nor a claim.'

'Tell me its name.'

                    'How can I? It has no name.'

At Vigna La Corte

hic in reducta valle

1

The floor of the path in autumn:
Crisping walnut leaves, cast chestnut husks,
The chicory flower blue on its stem,
White stones –
            A sheen on surfaces
Like a happiness
That cannot find its cause.

At the moment of striking the light draws away.
The things are shown and yet not reached.

2

Dusk: they bring the animals in.
The horses, for all their strength and size,
Are led by a small boy.

Turning into the road from the steep track
He stops at the parapet of the bridge,
Climbs on the back of one and sits astride.

The bridle rope coiled at his wrist,
He nudges the great flanks with his heels.

The Pool

There is no reflection on the dusted surface.
An edge of lime crusts the steep rock. Some leaves
Lie on the water. A frog leaps from your tread.
A trickle spills and seeps away through gravel.

Come back in spring to bathe here.
Winter will bring the pool back to its shape.

A Greeting

Small boy watching the pigs turned loose to root
In the rich grass that grows along the stream,
You greet me easily. What I hear in your voice
Is that the grass and water are as surely there
For you as for your animals. You are happy
In the sunset that picks out the hillside with shadow –

There is a fine intelligence in your eyes.
What I love is that it does not disturb
Your standing quietly among the things you know.

At Midday

When at midday, full of heat and sweat,
I leave my work and lie in the cool,

You are diving and hauling your body wet
Into the sun from the valley pool.

'Nothing but the flicker of leaf shadow'

Nothing but the flicker of leaf shadow over the dry streambed,
Small insects visible in the sunlight, mossed rocks and roots.

In the open meadow that you come on from the forest path
The cropped green does not mind you, nor the fading bracken.

Child, here you are as separate as the hunter but without
The hunter's purpose. Instead there is your body's wish.

You are alone with it among the rosebushes red with hips,
The white stones, the bramble patches, the stray birdsong.

For Pasolini

Vecchio ragazzo di Casarsa, dear protagonist,
Where shall we find the like of your intelligence?
The hunters who come here on Sunday with their dogs and guns
Are not enough to keep the forest paths open.
Two years untrodden, and bramble will cover the track,
The broom lean across. They were paved once with stones
Packed in together to make rough and narrow highways,
Loosened now, a rubble, a watercourse, except
For some short stretches where the old work has held.
If someone climbs up between the crests of the ridge,
Pushing through bracken that drenches his boots and clothes,
He will guess perhaps that this was the charcoal-burners' place:
But who can imagine now what their lives were, find more
Than that if he scratches the surface of the mounded green
He turns up blacker earth – their trace? O early bodies
Moving amid the dark as it thins, O quiet voices.
When ignorant beauty chances to conjure back to life
The shape present in the air, who will be here to know it?

Derelict Landscape

The rock that has broken and toppled across the track
Where cattlemen drove their herds will never be moved.

The manners of the old men coming in from the fields
At nightfall are sweeter than the bodies of the young.

The Last of Summer

1

What shall I find in fields running to waste?
        How fix the care
That stirs in me, aimless as autumn air –
Without an object but the sweet white taste

Of hazelnuts, or blackberries, the last few?
        And then to sleep
For half the morning, shepherd without sheep,
Stretched where the early sun has dried the dew

And in some nook its delicate warmth is held.
        The thoughts that I
Tried to brush off as daydream, fantasy,
Destructive of the nature I had willed –

I let these in; with them, the recollection
        Of how my shame
Was shot with beams, withdrew till it became
A mutual joke, a part of shared affection.

2

Enigma's place, the hollow among boulders –
        The old demand
Which drew me back repeatedly to stand
Where the stream broke about my head and shoulders

In stifling plenty; the cold shock, the sense
        Of boundaries
Reached and restored, the supervening ease;
– Proofs of a kinship between elements,

The world's, my body's, which importunately
        Required its due:
All these composed a rite supplanted now
By a stronger claim, a nearer memory.

Needless for me to look for what will come
                Without a greeting
In its own time. Time enough, at that meeting,
To crouch beneath the onrush, battered, numb.

3

Chirr of cicadas, the always-running stream,
                The heat-filled day –
As far as the land reached, these reached away.
Each day labour would make me one with them.

Existence through effacement! Anything less
                Seemed less than life
To me. I felt the pull of the world, as if
The senses were a sum of consciousness

Claiming me fully. What they could not gather
                Into their trance –
The faults and griefs – was mere inconsequence,
Theirs the whole story cancelling every other

Without a hearing. Yet the whole story none,
                Or what was told
By water in its course, will-less and cold;
By spots of sweat fading on sunwarmed stone.

4

Squat mounds of bramble cast their shade,
                Marked out with dew,
Across low turf. The track's brown curlicue
Climbs to thyme-scented slope and broomy glade.

Hazel and blackthorn skirt the stream –
                A trickle still,
Running in its grey cranny from pool to pool.
Between dry stalks spider-threads drift and gleam.

The meadow in the slanting sun
        Shows as it was,
But changed invisibly to leavetaking's place,
The mastering fullness of the summer gone.

I'm claimed by a gentler revery,
        A kinder embrace.
Love's smile, which can't be kept out of the face,
Is what I come from and what waits for me.

Autumnal

1

The water (that soon will raise its undertone
To a funnelled roar) trickles across warm stone.

2

Only so far you accompany the year:
Let it go on alone now, leaving you here.

Seasonal

Wrap up warm. The year goes down to winter.
A cold air stirs. The body reclaims each sense.
    No further your protracted dream prevails
Of a consciousness shared with the elements.

    Time to fetch the wood in, to light a fire,
To roast the gathered chestnuts; impatiently
    To wait until spring visit you again
With the thought of what full nakedness might be.

Pastoral

The web of mist across the morning
The rusted vine-row heavy with grapes
The chicory flower blue on its stem

Casual variety of a world
Which through the pain of labour I tried
To gather into a single thing

The empty meadow in slanting light
The hedge-gaps closed off with bundled thorn
The bramble-mounds casting dewy shade

A single thing a limitless thing
A vision which possessed and dispersed
My sense making it all and nothing

The smooth lip of the hidden gully
The moist pliancy of stalks of broom
The dark pool with its shivered surface

If all and nothing mine no longer
What was there for sense to return to
An aimless body in squalid fields

The mint filling the air at my tread
The grey glitter and rush of water
The spun threads astray between dried stalks

Shadowtail

Sudden across the path,
A black squirrel –
Morning's luminous shadow!

Summer Noon

Theatre of hills –
An audience of cicadas
Applauding summer.

★

The blood starting
In a fine column
From the mule's flank
– A horsefly bite.

★

Hung in a treefork,
The viper's drying carcase
Eaten out by ants.

Autumn Night

One star through the cloud
That drifts more thickly in. Far off,
A chained dog moans.

★

A moonless darkness –
Water and air no longer
Extend their welcome.

★

I sleep unwashed and warm,
Sheathed in the honey smell
Of hay from the stack.

Summer

The cold will-less muscle
Of water pushes at my hand.

The grass moves in the sun,
A floating pell-mell of shadow.

Osier Bank

Under willow bushes
A dewy hollow –
The air still fresh at noon.

A Storm

A meadow afloat with white campion, wild parsley;
The hill-ridges grey now with sunlit shadow –

What to do with this beauty except stay for it?
But I up and run from the lightning's pale flare.

Broken Weather

Ants drown in windfall
Apricots. Through loosened air
The stream sings its waste.

Outside

He walks down from the village,
In his brain its words and gestures.
A boy on the road shouts after him
Pointing a jovial finger at the sky,
'*Cammina... se non...*' but he walks slowly

Wanting the storm to break, to open
The wide shepherd's umbrella,
Road and river to be set awash
Like smears of shining ash
Till the land is ghostly –

After Football

They come to water
As if the flesh at its most live
Should find its proof
In that cold touch,

The stream welling
Over their forearms,
Lifted to their faces
And across their slight chests.

Contadino

I am not these: stones, a handful of earth,
Water with some dust on the tip of its tongue.

I am the length of two extended arms,
Hitched to the dryness of effort in my throat.

Hill-Path, Meadow, Cascade

1

Crushed rock, torn roots, trickling earth –
The hill-path bulldozed out.
                                    I follow it,
A stranger, missing beneath my tread
The old configuration of stones.

2

A smooth meadow. The swallow's low flight there
Accompanies its shadow. Grey amid green,
A heap of stones lies weathering,
Undisturbed since the first clearing of the ground.

3

Beneath the noise
(Like rocks knocking together)
Of water as it plunges –

A hum, a thin stridency,
As if a trapped column of air
Shook in fine vibration.

Orchid Field

Greenwings – purple lamps
Making their own light
In the shadow of a briar.

The Valley

The barrier through which the body has to fight
Is the body, yours and the world's. Time and again

It emerges beyond itself, transfigured, lightened,
Yet at a loss; as when, climbing past a ridge,

You come out above the head of a trackless valley
– Yours to gaze over, pleasant in the morning sun –

And, caught in the promise of its light and shadow,
Stand with it at your feet but do not go down there.

Alone

This was the most familiar
prospect: figureless landscape

in which no hope might gather
itself to a human shape.

At Moonrise

Youth's good was its own body
Which did not fail.
At moonrise I would dive naked
Into the pool,

Splinter the beams, surface,
Watch them regather.
Self-knowledge was no more
Than the touch of water.

Vintage

Could we set it aside,
　　Withdraw our hands
From grape-harvest, the task
　　In which we share,

To reach for each other!
　　I cannot rest
Merely in your presence
　　And my own thoughts.

I look from the vine-leaves
　　Where my hands search,
To your face, to the way
　　Your body leans,

And then down at the soil,
　　Cast where the plough
Has turned it, and crushed mint
　　Flavours our steps

Like a wish in common –
　　Yes, to lie there
With the dry grit pressing
　　Against our skin.

The Bathing Place

The body, wearied by labour, weary of
The clothes in which it laboured, puts them off

To loiter here, unhidden and unalarmed,
In the security of nakedness.

Hang-Glider

Earthbound we gaze, astonished and unfated,
Like shepherds from the fields where their flocks feed,

At the great morning where you hang translated,
At once an eagle and a Ganymede.

Bather

Where the dry gully yawned,
its boulders agape,

now water pours...
You stand above the cascade,

facing the hills,
yourself their embodied shade:

an expectation
freed into human shape.

On the Same

Swimming, I watched you stand on the concrete shelf
Which spans the torrent;
                        and, as I felt myself
Dispersed, could see you take on identity:
The hills came up to your waist, then there was sky.

Diving In

A bobbing headpiece merely, my body lost!
The surprise was to be suddenly so low:

The prisoner of a net fluidly cast,
Which held in its perpetual letting go.

Torrent

In hollows of the stream-bed the air lies cool,
Though summer has long dried up the deepest pool.

Here, when late rains and the dog-days briefly met,
Quick bodies would dive and play, brown skin gleam wet.

A Last Look

The enigma gone!

Do I care about the despoiling?
– The rape of the riverbed
For gravel,
                    its change
To stagnant shallows,
Reaches of pale mud:

An impure wilderness
Where no way opens
For water or feet;
                        unlearnt
The paths' good sense,
The logic of the streams.

Further Notes

Stunted oak coppice,
The stiff russet leaves as yet
Undislodged by buds.

★

The mule rears forward
Clumsily, after new grass –
Its front legs hobbled.

★

A shower that stings:
Unripened olive pellets
Pelting in the gust.

★

Above low black hills
A dust of light in the sky:
The moon unrisen.

★

Leaves, very gently
Moving over each other
To learn what shade is.

★

Still working their way
Out of each palm, tips of spines
From gathered chestnuts.

At Ponte Margheruta

1

Your fierceness was rough and dry
Like summer stones
On the derelict path.

2

The walnut trees
Are casting their large leaves.
A cold air touches you now.

3

Slight entity,
It is your poem, as it was,
As it will be yours.

4

Greet me. Your voice
Comes from before damage.
In your freedom I am freed.

Youth

Youth, suddenly recollected, means this still:
To watch the weather coming over the hill

And feel, though an unbeliever, dread or love
Raised up in me by a black or smiling Jove.

3
Monte Gennaro Epigrams

the custom'd hill

Epigrams: One

The Pool

1

What can the water be, other than itself?
I thought it was a fate gathered from the hills,

From each grey cranny, each hollow of moist air,
To glisten on your shoulders, your narrow chest;

And I imagined how you would turn in sleep
In the dark barn as the dream took hold of you,

Its weight and plenty bearing your body down –
A wish disguised, a knowledge not to be kept.

2

The land took everything that was there to take.
What remained was what was unpossessible:

Servitude's counterpart, a hidden freedom
Ghosting your gestures, bringing you to the pool

To learn its own existence over again –
Your weightless body finding in the water

A different poise, the water as it clothed you
Startled alive to its cold buoyant plenty,

The Day

1

Slow climb through darkness to the upland pasture,
Gathering the cattle, driving them to water,

Then down again as sunrise touches the peaks –
Each moment brings its patience. But first this pause:

In the low barn you take an egg from the straw,
Pierce it with a matchstick, stir it, suck it down.

The stars are sharp still, the mountain-ridge seems near.
Freed of its chain your dog whimpers to be off.

2

At nightfall a cold gust shakes down walnut leaves
On the gravel of the roadside as you pass.

Open it for me, the day which your voice holds –
No scared acknowledgement but a full greeting,

Young and clear-spoken, that cherishes its vowels;
Ancient exchange, trace of the hidden city

Whose derelict ways are there to follow still,
Your steps treading back the bramble and the broom.

The Men who Built the Paths

Their shouts bounced off the cliffs, they drank at the springs;
Like flesh from bones they have melted from the land.

They are still with you, the men who built the paths –
You rest in their given unremembered strength.

The Paths

Of so much building and passage, what remains?
The ghost of an old patience revivified,

A lost language that looks for a living mouth…
The new-made body – its effort and desire –

Waylaid, abstracted, among coppice and broom,
On cyclamen slopes, beside moss-bearded walls

Where paths run silted with oak-leaves, chestnut husks;
Tacked wire grown into the bark of trees, the wood.

Morning Moments

1

Trees start to break from darkness and waternoise.
Low mist cobwebs the valley. You look across

To the hidden meadow where your horses graze,
The dew-charged air pricking at your face and hands.

2

Early light. The heavy figtree by the path,
And your word of greeting from the dew-soaked field

Like fruit that is ripe but chilled by the night air,
Concealing something of its taste from the mouth.

Sunrise

Your face still blurred with youth; and the valley-floor
A space that lightens from black through grey to white –

Meadows and stables, riverbed, walls, trees, paths,
Hidden, half-hidden, as the mist thins and shines.

'I had no way'

I had no way of desiring you except
That you should be there, standing under the vines

In the grey of morning, work not yet begun.
I thought that you belonged with the early light,

Calm, uninsistent. But when the sun came up,
Edging above the hill-crest, blackening the hill,

The liveliness hidden in you, quick and sharp,
Made you one with the first beams needling the air.

Hillside

I enter derelict barns, twist myself round
The trunks of broken trees, follow unused paths,

Stand on the sunny ridge where the cliff falls sheer
And on the moss-grown scree at its shadowed base.

I wake past midnight with the moon full on me,
Lighting a musty emptiness in my head,

And walk, as if fated, into the dark air
To take my station against the hill's black edge.

The Bathers

1

The bathers at their ancient, always renewed,
Never-enough-repeated experiment:

Momentary synthesis of heat and cold
In the integrity of full sensation.

2

Seen from a distance, touches of brown through haze:
They wait on the concrete shelf above the pool,

Unwilling to leave; though, with the afternoon,
The further hill-ridge turns brittle, shadowy.

Storm will involve them as it sweeps the valley
– A premonitory gust through willow scrub,

So that they shiver; then the first scattered drops,
Heavy and sudden, pockmarking the warm dust.

Monte Gennaro

Cut-out marks of a child's toy, the stars hang low.
In the morning the word-giving mountain smiles.

Epigrams: Two

Two Hill-Pools

1

The noise of water, shutting out other sounds,
Has drawn him down from the hill-path to the pool.

A tense complicity brings him here to bathe.
His body is never more itself than now,

All feeling gone except for the buffetting
Cascade, a dissolving screen across his eyes.

What is it that he is left with? What survives
The torrent's numbing onrush and pulls him clear?

2

Again to meet it. Turning aside at dusk
Where path and streambed cross, to follow the stream.

Waylaid by an old temptation or belief,
He stumbles along the deepening corridor

To find – what is it? – something live but other,
And his body's recognition startles him.

The wide ripples push out from a thin cascade,
Green, white, pale. A colour that he cannot name.

Ruined Shrine

1

Cliff-rooted oak coppice, slopes of thorny brush,
Thick forest, sudden lawns close-cropped and dewy,

Heavy curtainings of lime-encrusted moss
– As if a city were overrun with green.

Here the dead keep him company; their language
His to recover, the good sense of the paths.

Where the track is overgrown he feels it still,
A level, a direction, beneath his tread.

2

A grassy cattle-pen on the hill's shoulder,
Some tumbled blocks lying among broom and bracken

Strewn down the slope. Surface by weathered surface
He searches out their vestiges of design,

Like clues to a language that might be reclaimed,
In a portion of its sense, from some few words –

A curved fragment of cornice, a grey rosette
Curling its petals for the finger to trace.

The Spinney

1

Berries still catch the sun on the brambled bank.
The coolness draws him in. He turns from the path:

In the grey pool a litter of sticks and leaves;
A couple of figs, fallen. Picking these out,

He tries their cold unripeness on his palate
As if they were a charm which brought admittance

To – what? He pushes past a curtain of briars
Along the stream-bed, over lime-crusted stones.

2

Above his crouching steps the spinney closes,
And whether the fateful hope prove mere caprice

Is not to be settled. He will re-emerge
None the wiser except for a scratch or two –

On the green pediment no bright appearance
Discerned, no god in the torrent-worn recess.

Not far is far enough on the nameless track,
Its secret no more evident there than here.

Panic

Swift sky, snow-crusted boulders, brown oak-coppice,
Dry leaves waiting dislodgement. Then he heard it,

Out of the air beside him a long-drawn groan
As if a body were turning from its wound –

What wound? In terror he plunged away and down
Till he found a path. There was a bridge below,

Its arch of smoothed stones evidencing a life
Perfectly fitted. And yet such room for fear.

The Stream

Pouring of water through the night, through the year,
The last sound before sleep, the first on waking;

Transparent path, almost overgrown beside
The trodden path's embankment of earth and stone;

Clear-bodied wholeness at the field's edge, logic
Finding out the lowest place, the easiest way;

An elemental beside a human sense,
Where he kneels to drink, to paint his skin with cold.

Bather and Horseshoe

1

Spring weather; days of alternate storm and sun.
Pausing at the bridge, he looks aside to where

The torrent spills from a concrete breakwater
To flood a hollow scooped in the bed below;

And sees – emblem of a pristine completeness –
A bather standing among the willow scrub,

Gentle and exact, feet curded with the dust,
Letting air dry him; who turns, then turns away.

2

Burst walls, rough fields, the dilapidated path:
Among loose stones the fragment of a horseshoe

Scraped thin and bright at the edge, one rusted nail
Adhering still. Picking it up, he studies

The fine pattern of scratches on its surface
As if some meaning which he could not construe

Were to be found engraved in the worn metal;
And thinks again of the figure by the pool.

The Last of Monte Gennaro

One detail only, still to record – the spout
Of split bamboo set in the stones of the spring.

4
Sabine Portraits

Continui montes ni dissocientur opaca valle

Antonio

Once you had checked your cattle and taken them
To water under the shoulder of the ridge,
You searched around the clumps of broom and bramble
– The ungrazed places – for wild asparagus,
Your brusque hand pushing aside dry briars to pluck
The fine stems that would flavour your midday meal.
Then back to the village by the well-known path
Followed day after day – the broken turf-bank
Swept in May by a flight of yellow orchids,
The sandy defile, more watercourse than track,
The close-paved stretch before the broad loose descent
Into the valley; and between dry-stone walls
Smooth from the riverbed, past orchard, stable,
To your own door.
                          Wouldn't these things sustain you
(Being as much part of you as you of them)
Against the old sickness that came back to dog
Your middle-age: a weak chest, breathing troubles,
A winter that you could not find your way through?
Since I can see you still, breaking off your search
Across the slope and approaching with a smile,
The bunch of wild asparagus in your hand.

Franco

The stable at the road's bend (asphalted now,
Once a rubble of white stones);
                                  and you still there,
Calmo, lucente, standing by the doorway
In the early sun, ready with your salute:
A slow good-morning, vowels drawn out as if
There were substance in them to last the whole day

– Though killed in a bike-smash thirty years ago.

Giovanni
Recollections of the Mill

1

Once the miller had driven off in his trap
To market – he would be away till nightfall –
The boys, waiting and watching at a distance
As the morning's early heat intensified,
Would gather by ones and twos behind the mill
And strip and run out along the *vasca*'s edge:
The walled pool whose collected weight of water,
Coldly brimming, lay idle and unguarded,
Theirs all day long to dive and splash and play in.
Nineteen-sixteen. War was a havoc elsewhere;
Faintly its loud heroics reached the valley –
It could not touch the bathers at their pastime.
Hard now, Giovanni, to think you shared those days,
That trance of quickness and anonymous youth,
Since you so steadily bear so changed a part
In these!
              Resting the mattock against a clod,
You hitch your trousers amply about your waist,
Then, fondly garrulous, push your black hat back
To wipe your forehead and broad grey-stubbled face;
Still working ground in earshot of the millstream
(Your daily bottle of wine laid there to cool).
The stream runs down between briars and willowherb
Across the *vasca*'s silted floor, to vanish,
Gurgling, through metal bars in the far corner.
Mirage of unspent plenty, this other view
Wavers in the warm air between vacant walls.

2

Wartime again. A squad of Germans stationed
In the valley, bored, impatient to be gone –
Their job to guard the road over the mountains
While a retreat continued by other routes.
A young man of the village, a friend of yours,
Stole two oildrums from them. The theft discovered
And the thief known, he ran off into the maze
Of hillside paths and meadows. There he found you.
You stood with him in the high fields debating
– Two innocents, sharing their indecision:
Should he go down? He could hear his family
Calling from below, telling him that the drums
Had been handed back, that he was in the clear.
At last, not thinking that much, if anything,
Would come of it, and hoping to brave it out,
He'd gone back down.
                              The soldiers found and brought him
(Devoted victim for whom their grievance craved)
To an annexe of the mill they'd commandeered.
I had seen it once, though shut up since those days,
A room drearily derelict, with paint-splashed
Discoloured walls and sour dust-coated lumber.
At the far end there was a narrow fireplace
And, built above, a kind of open chimney
Furnished high up with hooks – a handy gibbet.
From this, next day, burnt, beaten and cut about,
His body had been found hanging by the heels.

Giuseppe

When *rocca stupida*, flaking easily
Beneath our picks, gave way to *rocca viva*,
Its blue-grey crystalline percussion bouncing
The steel back up, we called for you, Giuseppe:
You placed the gleaming wedges, swung the hammer.
So it was, whenever a singular act
Of strength was called for; so it always had been –
Until the arc of the hammer brought you down,
Burst your heart.
                Yours was the *cruda senectus*
Which Virgil attributes to the Ferryman;
It carried you over quickly to the shades.

Maurizio

1

When you crouched, mallet in hand, on the roof's edge
Whacking at the obdurate rim of concrete
To be broken for the placement of new tiles,
I stood at the apex, protesting, my face
A study in redundant concern,
                      until
You glanced back and good-naturedly silenced me
With your reproach, '*Eh, la pelle è mia!*'

2

'*L'aria è sincera*' –
                the words spoken
Of the clear dusk, unwittingly of yourself,
As you looked up from the part-dismantled roof
At the sky beyond Lucretilis,
                  to judge
If the tarpaulin should be unrolled that night.

Adamo

1

The road to the village turned back on itself
And leaving the valley-floor climbed round a hill
To planetree-shadowed *piazza*, white stone fountain.
Your makeshift encampment lay down a rough track
Before the turning, and toward the valley's head,
Between the riverbank and a shelving cliff:
A hidden stretch of ground with pens for horses;
Under the cliff, a hardly weathertight shack,
Its fabric patched together out of remnants –
Tufa blocks, odd timbers, corrugated iron.
There your mother lorded it over her tribe
Of indeterminately fathered children
(You were the second) and her summer husband;
Elsewhere, it was said, there were winter quarters,
A winter husband. Watchful and capricious
She seemed to me, incurious, sturdily wild;
Her life a routine scandal, her confinements
The indisposition of two days – the next
She would be up, cutting and carting firewood.
This was your home. When first I went to find you
To fix a day for our proposed crayfishing,
I was dressed up for dancing in the village;
One of your sisters, big-eyed and barefooted,
Tiny in her grubby smock, her nose unwiped,
Stared from beside you and reaching out her hand
Involuntarily, fingered my silk tie
In wonder at the softness, the bright pattern.

Ducking beneath its roof of leaves we entered
The riverbed, I following – and waded
Upstream, bent over to scrutinize the pools.
There crayfish hung by ones and twos unmoving
In still grey water out of the main current,
Or stalked invisibly, grey as the water,
Or scooted backward with a flap of the tail
Through a sudden clouding of stirred mud, our hands
Darting to take hold of them as you showed me,
Between finger and thumb, clear of the pincers
Behind the whiskered head, and lift them away,
Tail aflap and pincers impotently stretched
(You held one out, smiling at its vain flourish).
Vigilantly we worked the creeks and shallows,
Wrenched stones over with a crash and rush of sand
Where one might lie in the lee of an eddy
Or find a bolt-hole. Once you surprised a toad
Squatting ominously in its dank hollow
And pelted it with stones (as I would not have);
Once, arm thrust to the elbow in a cranny
Of the bank, you felt a snake gliding away
Under your hand, and started back with a shout,
'*Vipera, vipera!*' The channel narrowed
And steepened among boulders, beneath a scar
Which stood up, grey and orange, into the sun,
Closing the valley. We had a basketful
To be divided, and turned back with our catch.

3

What elements compounded our friendship's fact?
– That pleasant ease in each other's company
Which, given our unlikeness, we hardly knew
What to do with or how to find a shape for.
Your sister's gesture pointed at what we were,
You and I, or were in part to each other:
Characters who had stepped out of a folktale,
As I, in my finery, appeared to her.
Did I waken some hope of a wider world
Beyond the valley, which you might enter on;
A hope that worked as the counterpart to mine
In coming to the valley, for me the place
Where the world opened? Or an erotic hope
Which, if I intuited, I never met
Because I shared it and was afraid of it:
The dreamt-of further signal of affection
Each was unready to ask for, or to give?
Or were you simply, if robustly, lonely,
Shut out, a gipsy, where the village ended,
Because of your parentage and poverty;
The butt of a taboo which I, as stranger,
Knew nothing of or if I ran against it,
Was unconstrained by? Was it sheer difference
Which proved us brothers, lifting away the bar?
You were fourteen, I seventeen. Together
We stood at a threshold giving upon views
Not then to be teased into identity.

You met me equally, ingenuously
If shyly, holding back out of a courteous
Reserve. And I was hesitant too, in awe
Of the sought-for idol that I found in you:
A presence within the presence of the land,
Summing the land up, self-surrendered to it,
Quickening it through your lively agency.
That was my imposition. And it was true:
You offered the reality of the place
Which made you, body and mind – more palpably
Than if these had been the gift; receiving me
With an archaic decorum, natural
And solemn at once, as prince might welcome prince
Into his borders. But what stays with me now
(My need for such construction having faded)
Varies between the specifics and the myth
In a slighter, nearer, more elusive sense:
However the sun came down the valley-side
To touch the encampment's level ground, it was
The clear obscurity of the riverbed
Which figured your existence, the muted light
Of its low-roofed, winding, leafy corridor –
Chequer of shadow over water and stones;
Your adolescent *vita umbratilis*
Aptly finding a metaphor, a place, there.
I offer what I took from you, Adamo:
These lines must count as my late gift in return.

A Sequel

Shouldering your way along the crowded aisle
Until you stand beside me, your face swung close
To mine, as the bus turns into the valley,
You challenge me,
            '*Ma non mi riconosci?*'
Then, smiling, '*Sono diventato brutto?*'

Don't ask if I recognize you, Adamo.
I know you by the old ingenuousness.

Improvements

Where previously a squalid encampment stood,
Now stands the neat municipal slaughterhouse;
That squatting family gone, their animals,
Their makeshift patchwork of corrugated iron.

Who could object?
            But everything is tidied,
Or pillaged... Tidiness denies the pillage,
While pillage gives the lie to the tidiness.

Opposite the slaughterhouse, the rubbish dump!

Angelo Hang-Gliding

1

Your brother pointed you out, a tiny flaw
Above the mountain-crest at the valley's end.
He was proud of you and pleased I should chance by
To witness this, your feat of flight. I had stopped
Beside him, and together we gazed skyward
From the patch of low flat stony ground between
The river and road – a makeshift football field –
To where you floated, buoyed on the light and air
Of morning. Then, as if some proof were needed,
He fished the speaker of a walkie-talkie
From his coat-pocket and, sending out its call,
Handed it to me. A little sideways jolt
As the suspended dust-mote leaned to answer
The signal, and your breeze-ruffled voice came through.
Next, the redundant exchange of courtesies
Your brother wanted, and haltingly I made
My tribute of the astonishment I felt;
That done, you gave yourself wholly to the flight,
We to our watching, wordless, our necks craned back...

Strange to see you ride out over the valley
From that high rockface, a swimmer in the sky!
Through it your embrace reached on unhinderedly
To become the air's embrace of all that reached
Away beneath you – if seen far-off, yet known
Close-to; as if the element which you rode
Were a mind in which these things lay visible,
And you, adventuring there, its consciousness.

2

You seemed so lost to us, so independent,
Remotely poised at the far edge of the sky,
That, after the first wonder, it was easy
To lose myself in the dream of what you saw,
Thence in a further daydream, and forget you:
Hillsides of olives, roughly-furrowed vineyards,
Their stiff clods lying unburst between the rows,
Orti broken to powder by the mattock,
Slopes where white oxen delicately stumbled,
Wide meadow astir with horses; fields, paths, pools,
The village backed against its hill, the graveyard
Marked off by dapper cypresses, the river
Curving among its gravel swathes and willows,
The single metalled road turning out of view;
Then mountains beyond mountains...

                                      Stare as I would,
I momently forgot you, and looked around
To find you had drifted from my sight – until
Suddenly you were close and large above us,
Sweeping the treetops in irrevocable
Descent, and touching down on the football field;
Then, all at once, clumsily earthbound again,
Your harness stretched behind you, an afterbirth
Spreading its untidy skein. Now disengaged,
You came towards us smiling, and already
Talking technicalities with your brother,
Demanding that at once he drive you pillion
Back up the mountain-trail for another flight.

3

Further into the mountains and one year on
The accident. It happened late in the day;
Just time, you'd insisted, for another flight,
The last; the addiction grown by now so strong
That it was your grounded hours which you would count
As the lost interval, your airborne moments
As true, a reclaimed existence which must be
Unceasingly known afresh. What held you there,
Devices, laws, became a second-nature
Relied-on and neglected...
                          No matter which
Of many taken chances – some shift perhaps
In the evening air you'd failed to allow for,
Or overreaching error – sent you smashing
Into pine-trunks on the wall of that ravine,
Hanging you there entangled, spiked and broken,
All-but-unreachable. Into the small hours
They struggled to release you, to bring you down.
Then months of hospital. A partial return
To life, to the cramped room below the village
In which your long convalescence faded out;
So to the other image which, juxtaposed
With that of your morning flight, I keep of you:
Shuffling for exercise on the balcony
And calling down (but your voice a cracked whisper)
A greeting, then the standard anodyne phrase
You'd settled on, the one recurred to in hope
Or hopelessness, '*Pian piano si arriva!*'

La Risecca

1

I put aside an intruder's bashfulness
(The shouts seemed to start from the air about me)
And followed the narrow sandy track until
I came to the pool. A musty dewiness
Persisted. I could feel it in the shadows
And the slipping of the stream over the stones…
You came up to me and, quietly surprised,
Asked, '*Ma sei venuto a fare bagno?*',
Pleased that the pleasure might be shared but thinking
The place somehow too humble for visitors
– Scarcely indeed to be considered a place
Except for this brief overlap of seasons,
Massed water from the late rains pouring across
A smooth-lipped barrage into the pit below.

2

You were proprietary about the pool
And showed me round, a perfectly-mannered host
Concerned to instruct me in its qualities,
Where it was shallow, where deep enough to dive,
Then leading me to the worn turfy platform
On which I must stand. Diving and surfacing
I marvelled at the water's sudden extent,
Its buoyancy and plenty, spilling, brimming,
Light with the air taken with it as it fell;
And craned my neck back amid the turbulence
To see the circle of hills all the way round
At once – a bobbing headpiece, my body lost
In a compass of sensation spreading on
Immeasurably with the stream's reach and rush.

3

Strange too to be suddenly so low, head-height
At water-level! Become mere consciousness,
I floated at the valley's centre, carried
On the element which reached from every part
Of all that lay around; and reached out through it
From charged capillary to broad riverbed,
Imagining that I reached to every part.
The works and days which disparately made up
My presence, I possessed as a single thing
Uniting in the long-drawn spasm of cold.
As by touch, so by sight: wherever I looked
I could set myself, knew the ground underfoot;
At the same time scrambling beneath the rigid
Skyline and here enmeshed in the torrent's toils.

4

From under the pool's hollow side where the bank
Grew thick with brambles, willow and hazel scrub,
Their tight roots twisted in among smooth white stones,
A few dry briars pendent, I saw you standing
At the far end, the cascade scarfed about you,
Holding to the concrete shelf, hands lifted back,
Belly flexed, chest lifting as you caught your breath;
Then pushing off and swimming underwater,
Barred with ripple-shadows from the midday sun,
Dark hair adrift, your elongated body
Trailing its limbs: fugitive quickness, a stream
Within a stream – as, pliantly, weightlessly,
You curved up from an opaque green depth, across
The shelving floor of gravel through milky light.

The lesson was, there could be no intrusion.
In the democracy of air, water, place,
To which I had found my way, the visitor
Belonged, and was received, as a citizen.
What did I think myself (how an exception?)
That here I should be treated as a stranger,
The one whose presence must be accounted for?
My bashfulness now appeared as self-conceit
Of the wrong kind, and your proprietary
Delight as an instance of the proper pride
In which, newly enfranchised, I claimed a share.
Of that you did not speak, considering it
As common knowledge: what needed to be said
Of the expectation which had brought us here?

Castagneto

A wind-up gramophone among spiny husks,
'*Ti voglio ben assaje*' and '*Vecchio frak*':
Under new green we danced in the chestnut grove
On a dry floor of shed leaves. Below us, past
The trees and paved *salita*, the garden-walks
And low grey walls of the poet's ruined house.
If I had cared about precedents, I might
Have thought of his Lalage, of Tyndaris
Invited from the city. But I had eyes
Only for you, Gianna, Maria Grazia,
And thoughts only of you, twin Graces indeed,
The instigators and leaders of our dance;
As, easily smiling and with quick light tread,
You taught a hobbledehoy to match your steps.

Maria

Your clothes were the colours of the autumn hedge
By which I saw you walking, all yellows, reds.
But that was in a fable where we were still
Half-children – an illustration to a tale,
Its page open before me.
                              In the picture
We face each other, strangers who would be friends,
Shy at a first encounter. I'd watch for you
Coming up the hill-path among your cousins,
Through that season, to greet you and be greeted...

Then we diverged into our untouching lives.

Elisabetta

The old dog lifts his head, snaps at an insect;
Roused, attempts to get up, raggedly does so,
Hind-legs sprawling on the polished travertine,
Back hunched from lying, and pads across the floor
To find a cooler, more comfortable place.
Where would that be? Here, or else here? He noses
Beneath the curtained windows... Nowhere pleases,
And he collapses randomly, breathing hard,
With a muffled knock of bones, out of the sun
At least.
                  Sunburned, robust, Elisabetta
Follows him with her eyes, leaning on a broom
(Her sweeping interrupted to let him pass),
And comments, '*Ha bisogno della morte!*'

Near Civitella

A few sticks laid in melting snow, chapped fingers
Held out against pale flames. As I walk on by
The huddled boys call to me, pleased with their fire,
'*Vuo' scaldar un po'?*'
                  I don't remember now
What errand took me along that wintry road;
The phrase comes back, though, as if freshly spoken,
Its invitation still remaining open.

Licenza

You withdraw further, are lost to the mind's eye,
Sinking away into the path, the hillside,
The patch of dusty ground among willow scrub
By the valley-pool; and these too disappear
Like being young, like the lively contentment
That keeps its energy... my admiration
Gone with the scene where it had play, the river
No longer batheable, the paths repossessed
By thorns, by rockfalls. Who would need to pass there?
An aged used landscape! Let the process of loss
Go unrecorded. This is – this was – the place
Where expectation took on its clearest shape
And promise was most substantial, breathed alike
In the dew-shedding air of early morning,
Carrier of greetings; in the heat-crammed noon;
The passivity of dusk, at summer's end
Undermined by gusts of wind and colder dark.

5

The Trance

I knew that the trance must end,
That I would be found as before
Staring at the rutted earth
Of the track, at the leaves shifting
To casual gusts of air,

Deserted by enchantment.
But at noon, on the bright hillside,
In labour's interval,
I gazed at the landscape
And my senses were not mine.

My body was a transparence
Spread widely as my eyes
And closely as my touch,
Where what I saw and touched
Came to a sense of itself.

Nothing since in the world,
Neither effort nor ease,
Has allowed me to surpass
Or efface the lonely shape
Set in abstraction there.

Not the hectic pastoral
Of office, rented room,
And the blandishments of dusk;
Not you, even, gracious child,
Half-crushed in my embrace.

Morning

I watch the shadows of trees withdraw from the stretched field
Which keeps its dew, like the first modesty of nakedness.

If I look at this for itself, it is emptily beautiful.
If I look at it in your absence, I imagine you here.

'Runner, unwearied'

Runner, unwearied,
At the chariot wheel of the sun –

How you need reassurance, child,
When day has withdrawn.

Fantasy

We would have trembled with the secrecy of the place
As if, thirsty, we could hear the noise of water
With nothing to hinder our kneeling there to drink;
And have walked, the bracken reaching above our waists,
Some dog-rose petals cast large and white
Across the brittle remnant about our feet
Of last year's stems. Where the deer's hoof pushed at the soil,
We would have lain, with only the sky to know.

Two Shepherd Boys with Dogs Fighting

a picture by Gainsborough

1

I could put words into the mouth of the one
Who is panicked, and tries to beat the dogs apart
Until they whimper and cower. I know the rush
Of good intentions that invades his brain –
Indistinguishable from a rush of fear,
As with upraised stick he starts out of the wood.

As for the other, I cannot ventriloquize
What he might say. But his restraining touch
At the wrist of the one, his will-dissolving smile,
Are enough persuasion, whether or not he speaks,
To let the hectic impulse go, forget
The dogfight, and be drawn back into the shade.

2

You rush forward as if you were alone.
The arms that catch and embrace and pull you back
Are company. The touch that you did not seek
You yield to as soon as it finds you out.

What reason could there be to start away from it?
The dogfight? The muscle loosens in your arm
Even as you strain; your frantic head by his
That smiles to itself, half in, half out of shade.

Night Piece

You have freed me from the will's aghast attempt
To reach beyond itself, my lonely effort
On the unkempt hillside, in the empty house.

We move through pleasure, beneficent and shared,
Toward a necessity that neither hastens
Nor interrupts our voluntary approach.

What scenes come back, once that necessity
Is touched and we lie separately, cast loose
In the enormous dark! This room becomes

The world in which we have travelled and seen sights.
Here memory is gathered into consequence,
Taken from chance and made a part of us.

Bedsit in September

The small creakings in the woodwork
Around the window, and the touch
Of insects against the glass
Give way to the persistent noise of rain.

From the sink on the landing
Comes the scraping of a saucepan in water
Not hot enough to remove the grease.
Someone laughs on the stairs, knocks at a door.

What I listen for among these sounds
Is the chafing of the newspaper
Against the edge of your jersey as you breathe,
Lying on the bed and reading.

The Kites

On Parliament Hill that grey-skied afternoon
We watched the kites being flown. Out over the Heath
Each frail construction hung as if alone,
And single motionless figures stood beneath.
Which figure held which string could not be guessed.
The kites were anonymous and unpossessed.

It would not be like this, you said, at home.
There a family crest would decorate each kite,
And the sky would offer scarcely any room
As each strained to outride the other's height,
Tangling and intercepting in mock battle
Amid the confusion of the festival.

We stared at the chilly steadfast English view.
I thought of the need for open space, cold air,
Unsociably assuaged in me; while you
Were lost in your memory of India.
We both found unfamiliar company,
I in your crowded, you in my empty sky.

While Dancing

Suddenly he holds away from an embrace.
Can you read the thought as it slips across his face?
How present they are and how easily dispelled,
The charm of the dance and the love of the one held.

The Slope

Love's risky dealing –
I think of the ploughman
who ploughs too steep
or miscalculates the slope.

The machine goes over
suddenly (he must leap
clear or be crushed) –
over and over, buckling,

breaking into pieces,
till caught against the torn
bark of a tree
at the coomb's base

and left there,
beyond retrieval, rust
starting to discolour
the bared wood of the trunk.

Night Piece

Your sanity was my presence.
I lie here, safe, alone
And share your sleeplessness –

Imagining how the beasts,
Made tame by sympathy,
Range round you in the desert.

Bengal Nights

That was 'abuse'.
                    But you were resentful only
When your night-visitors, the eleven cousins
Older than you, drawn to your bed in turn,
Excluded you by day from their licit games.

Alternately the chosen one, the ignored one!
With what bland ease you succumbed, as if by right,
To that importunate cherishing, how gladly
Took instruction from its succession of whims,

I should have guessed, as innocently I played
The role assigned – honorary twelfth cousin,
Your refuge from the others;
                           and have known then
What grievance follows after the charm has failed.

Sybarites

The coin of our pleasure,
Its obverse face
Minted in high relief –

And its reverse?
The same type incuse, stamped
By the punch of taboo.

105

The Cookbook

A great-aunt's parting gift
when you, the pampered youngest
in the household, got your way
and upped and left for England:
a cookbook. You kept it with you
('I couldn't boil an egg')
from that first move, blue clothbound
boards soon stained by use,

its onerous directives
more loosely interpreted
as spices there prescribed
proved unobtainable
and new ingredients beckoned;
– a sibylline vade-mecum,
at last consulted only
fleetingly, for hints.

Heaton Norris, the late
'70s… Our idyll's
bolt-hole. Fondly absorbed,
you'd skin and quarter a chicken
while at your shoulder I'd stare,
illiterate, at the neat
blocks of Bengali script,
projecting on them – what?

Some humanist-imperial
fancy of far-flung truth
which I, by an act of soul,
might recover and translate…
'Pudding', 'Mulligatawny'!
Here and there the text
lapsed for a moment, mock-
heroically, into English.

It was the abstract shape
of print on page – its promise –
that captured me: a blank
which, as I quiz it now,
opens on nights and days
in that sour musty flat
where for a year, occultly,
we dispensed with time and place.

Harangue

You bowed before
the well-appointed certainties
in my rhetoric of reproach,
and listened to the sound

with the attention due
to an unshareable creed,
its heavy dictates
lost on your unbelief.

What you heard rather
was a conqueror's innocence,
comic and enviable,
lending me crass strength

– a notional safety
in which, through me, you might rest,
taking for solid ground
the black space open beneath you.

To Let

It was a mean flat –
you wore your entranced smile,
as if the humble, impossible
requirements of your dream
were answered there
          (humble indeed
beside the huge unauthorized triumph
the dream foretold).

The opaque screen
between your fantasy and the world
had lifted, and in its place
a fragile transparency
lightened your face, taking away
the enclosed look
in your large eyes.

                    ★

Communal, desolate, the hallway
– its payphone and loose tiles –
was lit through the porch's parti-coloured
glass (some lozenges missing). Privet
bushed out into the unmade road,
the unmown garden.
                    We
took courage from neglect.

Where softened Victorian brick had once
proclaimed a home a castle,
we were the squatting heirs, come back
anonymously, glad of a nook
to lodge
          our unhistorical joys.

Traces

The smile of the unrecorded –
to catch that was the mischievous
promise you held out,
the lure which drew me on.

Your dance threw off a foam
of movement, which dissolved
invisibly about you,
a trace felt in the moment

that it evaporated...
A boat's wake closing over,
a shooting star's brief track:
these were your metaphors.

Now this:
        darling and scapegoat,
you flourished, as if secure,
in the temporary shelter
commandeered by your charm.

Indus

The threadbare hand-me-down
of empire, your notion of the 'gentleman'
hid a code unsearchably
more ancient. Lying beside you

I reached out past our attic room
to a low flat-roofed mansion,
straw-rough walls, a bed,
a body that moves and moans –

remote scene of pleasure
conjured from a valley-town
whose bricks had melted back to earth
before any named event.

The Enjoyment

Two metaphors

1

You wriggled to evade; preliminary hurt
Welled into pleasure and you gave yourself up,

Arms and legs spreadeagled – beams of a star
Struck through its centre, bright resistance gone,

And the enjoyment, bearing you darkly onward,
Passed into nonentity (this, too, desired).

2

What smiling reaches the circuitous path
Led us through: high woodland, dew-matted lawns,

Waters to drink at and return to drink at!
We knew that we would emerge below the crest;

We would climb the mountain of our *jouissance*
And stand above it amid vertiginous skies.

A Blazon

To add an edge to pleasure, I'd startle you
With an account of what you were engaged on,
An obscene blazon whispered into your ear
Accurately phrased.
                    You were more shy of words
Than of what they named. Words netted the dark flow,
Constrained the simple offering of yourself;
Returned you, shocked and charming, to a sudden
Self-consciousness,
                    so made you doubly naked.

Stressed Syllables

For you the erotic was barely
involved with words (as it was
– intimately so – for me).

You preferred hints, teasings,
smiling periphrases,
sly clickings of the tongue.

Only *in extremis*
would you try ordinary terms,
as on the occasion when,

face down, with a small gasp,
complicit in subjection,
you murmured 'circumcised...'

– secret obsolete badge
of empire, sported by us
in our renegado game;

the two stressed syllables
timed to the two strokes
that quickened me to orgasm.

The Lake

Love was the dark lake in which we bathed together.
I stand on the bank now. You are drowning out there.

Five Sketches

1

'You must realize that I am very superficial.
I have been brought up that way – to talk
About this and that.
                                    This poet oh yes,
This general oh yes.
                                    Five minutes' conversation.'

                                    ★

I exhorted you to read 'about Indian history',
Talked of 'your culture'
– 'You should root yourself more firmly…'

Innocent words. You smiled at my hectoring,

And preferred the chat of the moment, the dance-floor:
To glide, leaving no wake;
                                    for fixity
(You taught me how to teach you)
To crouch, trapped fugitive,
In a submission which made you gasp and moan.

2

Your fantasy of annihilation
Was a joke to me. But when the girl's straw hat
Blew down between live rails
You jumped from the platform to fetch it
As if your life
                                    weighed as lightly as the hat
And handed it back, grinning,
Moments before the train hurtled through.

Was it this brave carelessness
Put paid to the attempt
To make an accountant of you?
                                    Certainly
You were no 'economist of your person'.

3

The pearl in the wine, my 'right gipsy'!

– And you kissing away
My Roman shock
                    at the improvidence.

4

A spring of failed exams, of tears;
A summer of 'could-be's', wishful hopes
While you 'sung and hopped
In meadows green' –

'And now green ice':
                    the bureaucrat's
Sleights matching yours, his guarded voice
And sly relish for the order of things;
Your passport returned, visa unrenewed,
Invalid,
          having been kept all year.

5

Tears – suddenly at the barrier
As we embraced, then uselessly
On the Terminal roof
As, unclean with fatigue, I watched
Your plane take off,
                    grow small,
Its steep thrust vanish in cloud;

And the thought
That for someone landing today
The story now beginning

Was the same story
                    over again.

A Likeness

Portrait Coins
of the Greco-Indian Kings:
turning the pages
I come upon a face
– your double's, clear
as in a photograph,
stamped in ancient silver:
a medallion head
from Taxila, full-lipped,
eyes deepset and large,
a hard expression
on features softly rounded
where disillusion
and suspicions amongst thoughts
combine oddly and cruelly
with generous feeling –
the trustful candour
of childhood still evident
in its opposite;
I recognize this
in him – this, and something too
of division suffered and relished,
a hybrid culture:
beneath the classic forms,
the inscription,
the moulding of the bust,
a different presence,
landlocked, indigenous,
swaying his look;
a further reach
of belonging than the Greek
(which was still his)
– Athena Promachos
from remote Pella
fighting on the reverse
but vainly...
and the Kharoshti
legend around.

Before a Journey

Where alders spring and a split hollow oak
Dies through hundreds of years, the quiet river
Makes slight sounds to itself like someone thinking.

The water has an unpolished silver look
At a distance. Nearby it runs transparent,
Shallow and clean over gravel with trails of weed.

Low fields, good for nothing but walking in,
Drenched grass that never dries through a winter's day:
These scenes are my whole comfort till I reach you.

Tufan Express

Washed-out brightness
of the saris
of field-working women;

the white dome glimpsed,
majestically elaborate,
above avenues of green;

a peacock agilely
managing its burden
of tailfeathers as it scuttles
across embankment and ditch:

what can these avail?

– sudden magnificence
ineffectual against
the meagre repetition
of plains, roads, hills.

Small-Hours Stop

As with the remembered journey, so with love:
We too travelled the ancient route, transformed
Its incidents into emblems.
                                    For example,
Our small-hours stop in that small silent town,
A staging-post between the plain and mountains.
Huddled among the crowd of passengers,
We sipped thick tea at a charwallah's stall
While the night-bus, its engine idling, waited;
Each of us cradling in a hand the rough
Earthenware cup, glad of its inch of sweetness
And eyeing the fire beneath the pot.
                                    Refreshed,
I strolled aside. Along the shuttered highway
The ground crunched softly, unevenly, underfoot
And, glancing down, I made out in the shadow
How, for some distance round, greyly apparent,
The place was paved and mounded with a vast
Detritus, where cup on cup had been let fall
To be trodden back to earth,
                                    as in a moment
Ours would be (the bus honking its summons),
Our passage counted with the countless others.

At the Hill-Station

A room at the hill-station, fireless, bare.
No view. The hills are lost in mist-clogged air.

Plenty of space, though, to walk up and down
Thinking of unfilled spaces of my own.

Hill-Station Souvenir

From shrouded vantage-point to vantage-point
The guide conducted us that fogbound morning,
Promising us the views that might have been.
We stared politely into the wall of grey,
Soft and unvarying. Finally he brought us
To a small terrace above a hidden gulf
From which we should have seen a facing cliff
(He gestured grandly) plunge sheer to the plain.
It was no day for the sublime. We waited,
Mist catching in our throats, curling in our faces,
In case the cloud should thin, and a stone edge
Show like a shadow – then filed back again,
You and I with the others.
                              At the entrance
Some vendors of eucalyptus oil stood ready,
Bottles set out on the instant. One, to prove
The purity, dipped a rag in the oil
And set light to it, then (having let it flare)
Pinched out the flame, leaving the rag unsinged.
We bought a bottle. I, without conviction,
Tried it that night on an ankle dully sprained
And woke to find the ache abruptly gone.
But that slight comedy of surprise is hardly
What saves the incident for me.
                                    It was the flame,
Bright, quick, open, contrary, loose, free,
Coming as if out of nothing, richly fed,
Welcome and warm, which startled me, and stays.
How it burned back vagueness and opacity!
– An image of the desire that was between us
Certainly; but the desire itself
A further recession within the metaphor,
Figuring the half-forgotten, the unimagined:
As we had seen, struck from its latent source
In watery diffusion, the gush of fire.

An Ending

1

My touch might try to cure
But its effect would be
Only to restore the dream
Toward which my embrace
Released you once,
                  the closer
That the freer in fantasy
You might wander, opening
Within my constraint
Like a flower to the air.

2

Open like a flower to the air,
A lily buoyed on the current in which it moves
This way and that, swayed by the slightest shift
Yet never turning its gaze to consider its movement;
Open like a flower
              to the air, to the air
Without question or doubt –

There

There the secret is shown, the unspoken spoken,
The hidden grief rejoiced in, the worry over.

There, of taboos, you will at last discover
That the most rigid may be the soonest broken.

There an old difference changes to a token
Of likeness – forcing you, high-minded lover,

Down from the cloudy reach where wishes hover,
Your pleasure focused now, your need awoken.

6

The Last Caliph

for Dick Davis and Afkham Darbandi

1

Quietly he watched the weighed eyes close
And the unhallowed presence intrude.
When the boy fell on the rug, he rose
In silence, his anger dispossessed

By kindness that took as its disguise
Ironic leave of each kingly mood;
Then stared at the scheme of paradise
In woven silk, and the limbs at rest.

2

The masterful whirls seemed metal grills
Of a great window, at which he stood
For a breeze from the spare-featured hills
To sting his eyes like a hint of dust.

But its life was fixed like summer air
Till he assented with gratitude
To the grace that broke the pattern there
In sleep's unthinking perilous trust.

3

Taking your challenge, one from their line
Is drawn, as flies by the smell of blood,
To feed his quickness on your design;
And hovers, thin-bearded, empty-faced.

Gentle warrior, accoutred knight,
Whose field is mired by a stream in flood,
You mock his coming; as if to fight,
That too, were an exercise of taste.

What reason is there? Each perfect shape
Rebuts its devil and is pursued,
Turns at a promise, half-wills the rape;
Then feels the unclaimed impulse burst

Its random confines, until that drive
Is the one proof that is understood,
With no thought but panic left alive,
No art except to believe the worst.

Virginity

Brittle, complete, and never something made,
No hard won recompense of casual harm,
It graced the body's peace and its alarm,
And glittered with the impulse that it stayed.

Waterfall

Wet air and shadow. But the healer's touch?
The water on his shoulders fell like stones,
    Forcing his body to a crouch
As if to break through flesh and lay his bones

In the black pit of rocks. He crept aside,
An awkward stranger, from the water's hearth
    And felt returning as he dried
The worry that had brought him there to bathe.

'Hardly dwelt in'

Hardly dwelt in, always at risk
Brought by the touch of air at dusk
Or water in the mouth,

– And the drinker kneels, hands on the wet rocks
And the labourer stands,
His forehead crisp with chill –

Conviction that the body was not framed
To search in human task or love
The likeness of its need.

*

You are thankful for the weight of the rock,
The colour of the leaves,
The water running over the path;

Forfeit gladly your partial being
To theirs, able to share
A sense of the last breath exhaled

By which they baulked existence,
That now are given to themselves
As objects dropped in space.

The First Thing

This walking alone
Is before either loneliness
Or company. It is the first thing –

And to set prints in the dust
That the dry cold at night
Will leave unstirred.

Islamic Shrine

near Hamadan

The road, winding through villages, ended there.
A stream ran down from the hills, as if to meet it,
    Between grey tumbled boulders.
Autumn: a pink snow-light hung in the sky.

Except for the shrine, it would have been no place:
A facade of threadbare brick, a dome still bounded
    By one line of blue tile,
Some planetrees near the entrance casting their leaves.

We looked down at the fields: pale crumbling earth
Where snow would lie for more than half the year.
    We jumped from boulder to boulder
Along the streambed, but came back to the shrine.

What is there to be said of the memory,
Which blurs and stays? As the afternoon darkened
    We waited an hour or less.
Without our knowing, it made a place in our minds.

Sassanian Ruin

near Firuzabad

Two play at chess
in the shadow of a broken dome,
the palace hall

open now to the sky;
intent each move
made in their dusty corner.

★

Headlong over the reeds
a herdboy dives
into the King's garden pool,

its taut surface
vibrating in the noonday dazzle
to his quick strokes.

Median Palace

in Luristan

A king over shepherds: here he built his house,
His columned hall, roof set with painted tiles,
　　The master of an acreage
As far as he could see from the towered walls.

By what trust or ignorance did he build and live?
We drink at the spring that fed his walled garden;
　　We watch the crested hoopoe
Strutting in the court where once it drew his eyes.

How firm they must have stood, the bulwarked rooms,
Refuge from sun and snow and the great sky,
　　Before the frail balance
Of circumstance was jarred, and shook them down;

A layer of ash which we brush gently clear,
A hillock, pale earth melting to pale earth.
　　Did he foresee the fall,
The strangers who would explain themselves by swords?

I turn the tiles up where the roof crashed in
And find an earthenware fetish, a foot,
　　Its sandal bound by snakes,
And a bronze pin capped by a staring head.

No Village Was Too Remote

the Iran-Iraq War

The roadside soft with dust, the threadbare hills,
The teahouse with its incongruous velvet couch,
The felt-capped boy stopping with his goats to stare:
Dusk drew these together in a frail coherence
As the moon rose, strengthening through deep-blue air.

In that dry numinous light, it seemed, the country
Lay changelessly far off, and the childish face
Unreachably open between domed cap and coat.
I count the years now to reckon the herdboy's age,
And guess the sequel. No village was too remote.

A Coin

I think of a coin I bought once
And gave away, not knowing how I valued it,
A greening copper relic of the Kushans;

Stamped on one side
The figure of a trousered king beside an altar;

On the other the God of the Wind
Leapt forward, bearded and naked, his cloak
Looped out in circles around him and behind –

The type of an energy
Which must run wild to bring itself to shape.

Bread and Brotherhood

in Luristan

He came out of the house with bread in his hand.
His mother had just baked it, as he told me
(I happened to be walking by); and, tearing
Half the strip off, he offered it with a smile,
The flat uneven *nan*, mottled with scorch-marks,
Still warm and moist in its first freshness.
                             We stood
In the dusty track before his curtained door,
Munching companionably and looking out
At the morning and the land, the nearby spring,
The grove it watered, acres of corn and beans,
Then arid pasture with clusters of black tents:
Encampments of village families, for whom
– A generation's stone-throw from nomadism –
The habit of mud walls and poplar rafters
Proved hard in summer, in spite of planted fields.

Off to one side and out of view, the *tepe*:
Our excavation all but finished, the mound
Of habitations sifted now, dug-down-through
Past layers of burning, resettlement, neglect,
To the first ground-plan, the original floor,
Its beaten earth uncovered and newly swept…
I'd stretched out there as if to claim possession.

His name was Karim.
                         True, we liked each other
Though hardly in a way that had been tested
Beyond good nature's limit; were the same age,
Had shared a season's labour. But that meeting
– Call it the moment of bread and brotherhood –
Comes back persistently across thirty years
In its first freshness, not as more than itself,
If vivid, scarcely a parable – and yet
The sum of what can humanly be hoped for.

127

Middle Age

The temples, lakes and islands; rooms and roads:
When we go wandering, soon there's too much
To gather into consequence. Our touch
Has brushed too many stones; too many gods
Have played the host to us and had their claim
Shrugged off. Old pockets, worn-out wallets keep
The bills and tickets. In a drawer, a heap
Of shells recalls a place, perhaps a name.

Youth's body, like a broken statue, lies
Deep-buried with the meaning that it gave.
We cast about for something we can save
By which to save ourselves; more blank than wise
For all the miles that brought us to this ground,
Uncertain of where value can be found.

The Fault

What Youth had cherished was the body's neatness,
   A separate competence to set against
The soul-defeating sense of incompleteness
   By which a deeper fault was evidenced.

At the Well

The coldness of this water reaches beyond
Your worry. The look freshens in your eyes.

A hornet settles. Two rapt butterflies
Sip what you spill. The well-head burns your hand.

The Pillar

In the Temple of the Holy Sepulchre,
Along a shadowed aisle, there stands a pillar
   Marked from head-height to floor
With little crosses, irregularly neat –

A host of them, each carved by a crusader
To witness his arrival, his vow maintained;
   For so much risk and road
No blazon beyond this anonymous sign.

Running my hand over the polished surface
As if to gather up a swath of journeys,
   I felt the crosses' edge
Under my palm and fingers, an enigma

Coolly unyielding. With this came the desire
To reach behind the emblem, along each route
   From pillar to homeground;
So to recover the content of the voyage.

                 ★

I had forgotten. Disgust shadows desire.
Another life is never safely envied.
   The knowledge once attained,
We shy away from what we needed to know.

A hair's-breadth separates the panegyric
From an art that seals in words what can't be borne,
   So that it won't come back;
Neutralized its capacity to distress.

This holding true of holidays and heroes
(As, how much more, of the plight of every day),
   What then of desperate souls
Cursed by deeds they had acted, suffered, witnessed?

How could I quarrel with the instinct to close
The journey off behind the destination?
     But, pressing these thoughts down,
My jealous admiration was what prevailed.

★

The old recourse: imagination's compound
Of memory and wish. To make the fiction,
     I turned on my own tracks,
Conjured the darkling shift of harbour waters

On late eves of departure, morning seascapes
A-glitter, glimpsed unvisited Cytheras,
     Shoaled landfalls, rounded capes;
Tawny deserts, colour of a lion's pelt,

Forests, lakes, rivers, marshes; cliff-hung passes,
Thin upland reaches, green becalmed expanses,
     Broad highways, breakneck paths;
Hill-huddled villages, plain-circled cities,

Far mountains, pale at midday, purple at dusk;
Skies crazed by lightning, rain-riddled, dull with snow,
     Tyrannized by the sun:
The gamut of weathers over land and sea.

★

What bivouacs, embarkations, bargainings
For passage, what fevers and recoveries,
     What respites and fatigues,
Incised and hidden here, might have been evoked

To witness the dizzy sum of pilgrimage?
Idleness under awnings, the creak of oars,
     Water lapping worked stone,
Dolphin-outriders crossing before the prow

130

As it lifts and dips amid the swing of waves;
On a rainy morning in some market-place
    A cup of sweetened milk,
A cake, and from the vendor, muzzy with sleep,

A young gratuitous smile; trust and distrust;
Promiscuities of bed and board and road;
    The one assured treasure
A life, in recollection, truly possessed.

★

'The past', I said, 'lives in us or not at all,
As, stumbling on its exclusions, we are forced,
    Each opening instant, out –
But out into a future cognate with it

And to be turned to as a source of knowledge
Which can make good the exclusions.' This once said,
    I felt my envy wane:
The slow accretion of crosses notched in stone

Stood in no contradiction with the instant;
Was itself alive with possibility,
    Fixed there as if in flight
And beautiful in its fortuitous shape.

I thought of birds taking off at a handclap
Or cracked stick, from a tide-washed river-island,
    Wheeling and scattering,
The great flood and the bright air spaciously theirs.

Paestum Quatrain

O sun at morning on the ruined town.
O parting, no abasement in farewell.

O light upon the temple's golden stone
Cut by the salt-edged air, a glowing shell.

Gran Sasso

Around the highest village, fields are ploughed
However pale the soil and frequent the stones.

Old habits huddle between old walls. The church bell,
Slight and unresonant, is a familiar sound.

Above the village, the final mountains lift.
Who climbs them feels his life thin out like air

And finds beyond the ridge a treeless meadow
Without a trace of history or occupation.

Then the summit, gross blunted rock that has shed
The last vestige of anything but itself.

The Fields of Self

The Fields of Self
Are removed and strange.
There shepherds wander
And hunters range.

There spring is tardy
And summer brief,
And autumn brings
Neither fruit nor sheaf.

Deep winter has shut
Those bounds in snow,
While harvest burdens
The plains below.

132

Hellenistic Torso

the excavations beneath San Clemente

With surprise I come upon you in this dank crypt,
Broken marble: a figure, half-man, half-child.

What place have you here among sarcophagi
And the otherworldly stare of vestured saints?

You kept belief for the world in which you were.
Your body is the conclusion in which you rest.

From the vanished head two braided locks of hair
Hang down across your chest. I breathe your breath

And imagine their slight chafing on your skin.
You would have felt it, however still you stood.

The Plane Tree

Beneath my branches Youth a moment stayed
Then moved half free, then melted back to shade.
Age loiters still, lamenting for the boy
Who trembled when the sun required his joy.

The Statue

I am the nakedness that ghosts the land.
The water from this chalice in my hand
Figures my soul, continuously shed
To harmonize the silence of the dead.

Aspromonte

A dry riverbed. Stumbling across
its sprawl of boulders, he does not guess
at the water that still runs beneath.

But he is near the sea. The first hills
go up on either side, steep orchards
with unripe plums, slopes of coppice oak,

a line of distant crests. From habit,
he forces himself on through the heat.
He does not guess what upland coolness

is there to meet him among big trees –
the air a live presence about him,
the water pushing through his dipped hand.

Leaving

His best shirt, faded by the sun and frayed,
Is slightly too small. Beside him in the bus
Sits an elder brother. They are going North to work.
Children, old women, have gathered to see them off.

After the wavings, when the bus is on its way,
The boy runs a slow finger along his cheek
And then the line of his lips, as if to take
A last cognizance of his childhood face.

Common Sparrow

A poisoned seed or knock from a windscreen: loosely
The slight body lies in the handkerchief.

I set you among oakleaves, turn you with a twig,
Ruffle your feathers and draw out the wing.

Bird of Venus, show me how you are made,
The markings that you were quick to hide. Your tail

And folded sides dark feathers edged with brown,
Your breast the colour of an uncertain sky,

The yellow patch at the base of your squat beak,
Your freckled top and cheeks of puffed grey down:

As if guilty of some cherished crime, I dwell
On these rarities and make my acknowledgement.

A Robin

Plumping your feathers you come close for company,
Peck at the bark of a twig, at a grain in mud.

I notice how pale it is, the grey patch between
The rust-colour of the breast, the brown of the wing.

Then you make off through a fallen willow's tangle
– Out across the striped alternation of ripples.

Leant against an ivied trunk, I stare at the reeds
That stand up, dry and faded, from black reflections.

Richard Wilson in Wales

His mind was a lake trapped in a mountain hollow,
A thin trickle spilling over stones to a river
That wound where in youth he tracked it, to Italy –
The fields where the Graces showed themselves and danced.
The mountain shuts out the view and dulls the water
But the clouds are touched with a remembered light.

Palm Leaves

Moulded in white plaster
on the chapel wall,

palm leaves – now no longer
martyrdom's symbol,

thank god, but as themselves
the more beautiful!

The Alfred Jewel

Wolf-mouth, enamelled face and golden fret:
In that fine pattern our attentions met.

I keep it from the years, our one shared day:
The little space where feeling was in play.

Chinese Dish

If the shore is set with trees that can be named,
Among them a stilted terrace and a shrine,
It is to create of the white emptiness
A slow river, and to place there a fisherman
In whose contemplation this scene exists – although
His huddled figure, his boat tilting in the ripples,
His line are the incidentals of remoteness.

Angel

Your message was your smile
When you were here. Away,

News given of you is all
The news you have to give.

A Photograph

A camera that distances and shadows,
    An ancient photograph – two boys
Pausing by water at the edge of meadows,
The bounds of home. One sits. One stands at gaze.

Beguiling them with trivia, a dream
    Delays their bodies, vague and still.
But the image in the scarcely moving stream
Is perfect and inapprehensible.

If Once

If once we were able to be clear
Of sleep immediately on waking

Like those birds, that first bird
Alert to the light's coming back,

We would be able to understand
What death is, and not be afraid.

The Icknield Way

He wakes to the sky's first pallor,
Has shed the sickness of sleep
Before gold hits the cloud.

Summer is the heavy hedgerow
By the path. At his shoulder
He carries its weight of green.

Sunrise

Thin warmth toward which the body turns,
By which it grows:
         O hardly there,

Child shot through with the first beams
Of sex, and shivering in the sun.

Epigram

Your god is the one that makes the ears of corn
Milky, when the wind is soft in the field.

Later it will blow over the cracked earth
With a dry shiver that is thirst's own sound.

The Knot

The knot cuts across however far
You cut back the wood,
A deep engraining. The figure moving there
Is not where your passion centres
But is a likeness of the shape
That itself moves inside you.

Do not hope to get away.
It is with you like the beat of your blood
And in your nearest moment before you sleep
The sigh in the ear
Against the pillow, though you turn
And turn away from the sound.

Departure

No escape as he lifts away, thirsting for the purer
Thinner air of the future.
                              An aeroplane
Over steepening cloud flies toward its shadow,
That rushes up to meet it –
Cuts in straight, and the wings streak with snow.

The Changeling

The fruit falls in the garden where he played
And loaded branches of the pear-tree stoop;
They throw across his room a net of shade,
Like old accomplices blackmailing hope.

He struggles in the darkness to break clear
And wakens from a field thudding behind,
His body bathed in warm springs of a fear
That wells unstinted from time out of mind;

And memory, like a compulsive hand,
Crawls in its trance toward the trapped events
– Too trivial, if reached, to understand,
Too faint to settle in some final sense –

Where, bending his reluctant gaze at school
Beneath its daydream, and at nightfall laid
Between the new sheets, grateful for their cool,
The child was imperceptibly betrayed;

A stranger to the genius of his growth,
An image fastened like a fern in coal –
O doubt that catches in the breath of youth,
O muscle gritting round a spellbound soul,

Too deep within the luxury of its mood
To waken from the prayer to which it bends.
O mirage glittering in the waste of blood
Toward this thirst. O too sufficient ends.

Three Oxford Poems

1 *Ragwort*

One day each summer I would come home from school
To find our alley newly stripped of its green,
Wild ragwort gone from crannies under the wall,
Neat cobblestones with no moss or grass between.

Moss, grass and weeds would gradually grow back
And the year make good what had been cut away.
But, naked, the alley wore a shamefaced look
Which touched me as if the want were mine that day.

2 *In the Meadows*

A landing-place, stone coping heaved by roots,
Steps down to water, two rustless iron rings:
Finding these, I imagined a river-journey
From the city to a palace outside the walls.

Cattle range in deep grass, trample the shade –
No building more than a barn ever stood here.
But clear in my mind as when I was a boy
The palace's shape and the courtesies it housed.

3 *Swimmer*

Swimming upriver between tree-walled banks
Through hidden reaches scummed with dust and blossom,

I felt the water's plenty, its slow movement –
A largesse I need never cease to give from.

The Bravest Jump
(Highgate Pond, 1976)

For Michael Schmidt
on his sixtieth birthday

The weekend of our first meeting –
Half our lifetimes ago!
                    Yet there you stand
Ingenuously at the door, publisher's bag
Over your shoulder, clear as ever
To the mind's eye,
                    the 'toughie' who seems a 'softy':
I should have been put wise to that,
If by nothing else, at least by the incident
Which comes back to me, a fresh impression
Stamped emblematically on those days.
How could I have failed to read it?
                    But memory
Retains it to be read, and I do so now.

We had crossed the dewy fields of Parliament Hill,
You, and I with Rana (woken
From our drowsing idyll by the mugs of tea
You served us, though our guest)
For the bathe we'd promised, which your enthusiasm
Held us to, in Highgate Pond.
                    Your guides, we brought you down
Past the deserted precinct of bathing sheds
(We were the first that day), and out
To the little pier and dour grey-rippled water.

Beside the pier, taller than the cloak of trees
About the Pond, a tower of girders rose
Four-square, and a ladder to the high diving-board
– Insanely high it seemed to us, and you made
Some jocular reference to that
As a challenge to be braved,
                    which we concurred in
Jocularly. No sensible man etc.,
But you were piqued, and meant it.

We should not have been startled, Rana and I,
In the first delicious moments of our swimming,
When having tried the pool you slipped out and away
And, as we bobbed beneath, reappeared to us
Stalwart and sturdy, standing against the sky
Way up,
            then as you had to, I see that now,
Hurling yourself out in a headlong jump
(Half-leap, half-dive, which was it?),
Crashing down into the water, and surfacing
Into cheerful triumph, the impulse carried through
Whatever the damage.

You walked slightly askew the rest of the day.

From near or far,
I've watched you doing something of the sort ever since:
Slipping away from the rest of us
And heading, with an evasive flippant remark
Or joke more edged
Than you pretend, always for the highest board
– The white-painted posts and ladder
Which we stroll past and ignore
Or treat as part of the furniture
(Lounging and leaning against them
To chat of elsewhere and other doings)
– The tower it never enters our heads to climb,
Let alone hurl ourselves down from;
Not out to punish ourselves on holiday
With dares and tasks.
                        We're not that kind of idiot.

You are and have been, for all our sakes –
To see the possibility and to go for it
Being one and the same to you: no 'nice idea'
To be played with, then put aside.
Your banter is dangerous, full of intention,
Your hand already on the rung.

If elegance and accuracy have not been
Your consistent priority – as you'll surely allow –
Though often and happily attained in passing,
Neither have you sheltered behind them as an alibi
Preserving you from engagement.

The splash, when it comes, can be tremendous.
But whatever the comment of poolside loiterers,
Mere bobbing heads, treaders of water,
You know, as they do finally, that what counts
Is to have climbed and leapt;
Such faults as they may have captiously observed,
Following directly from the headstrong virtue
Which drives you,
                          as on that morning,
To make the bravest jump from the highest board.

At Old Hall

for Peter Scupham

Shepherds still follow their sheep where Hesiod
Once met the Muses stepping out of the mist.

(I conjure the place: wooded slopes and a path,
Hammocks of meadow slung between rocky crests.)

Are they to be met, too, in our lowland fields,
By our slow rivers, the Waveney or the Loire?

Down here they need a lower roof than the sky.
Where should they shelter but in your open house?

Mr Thewes

for Fernand Benhaiem

The Jewish lawyer from Constantine and I
Sit in a Blésois café, in bland exile,
Over morning coffee, as he recollects
His English *prof* at the Lycée, Mr Thewes,
The first foreigner whom he had ever met:
How good-natured he was; an outsider, both
Where République and Rabbinate were concerned,
The settled proprieties of school and home
Suspended in his lessons; how his story
(To teach the risks of mispronunciation)
About the finical lady who confused
'*Je me lave le cou*' with '*Je me lave le cul*'
Delighted the class – he had '*l'esprit Gaulois*';
And how he would caress affectionately
The curls of the ill-fed, unprepossessing,
Excitable boy, winning him on to learn.
'*Il était sensible à ma pauvreté…*'
'*Il a vu que j'étais un bon élément…*'

War came and with it a new term. In class now
No Mr Thewes. Then the word came he was dead,
Killed, how and where not reported, a young man
Not twenty-six yet. Three months later the boy
– Excluded ('*On ne peut pas, il est doué…*')
From the Lycée, under Vichy – had gone too,
Not understanding either loss, but sensing
That they must be connected. Sixty years on,
Mr Thewes is recalled '*avec peine*', the words
Heavily spoken and repeated, the grief
Fresh in my friend's face; with a grateful fondness
Both for the man and an imagined England,
Suggested to the boy by his courtesy
And kind regard. His memory, pushing up
Against the odds I think, like the one grassblade
Through asphalt, noticed by me in the pavement
As we pay and leave –, greenly raises itself
To show in our conversation and these lines.

Old Boy

Your name under *Deaths*
in the Old Boys' Newsletter –
last seen when we were twelve!
Precocious then as now,

you were first among us
to have reached and crossed
the sill of puberty.
We were impressed,

in the changing-room,
by your shadowed nudity,
the sex heavy-hung
in its thicket of hair

– too grave a sequel
for our jokes to master,
much less disown;
since, late or early,

shamefaced or immodest,
which of us was exempt?
Decently unabashed,
you merely showed the way.

No time. A lifetime.
The random image
of your fresh ripeness
(perfectly retained)

finds its place now,
clear of intervening
vicissitude, beside
this bare announcement.

The Thirteenth Book

When pious Aeneas got fetched up to heaven,
It was not a moment too soon. He had grown sick
Of his household gods with their incessant demands.
After the years of trouble to find them a home
Why couldn't they sit on the proper shelf in peace,
Not jostle angrily there, invoking the fates
And calling out (spoilt brats) for further sacrifice?
There would be no more rising to the occasion.
That final combat had taken it out of him!
Had no one stopped to reflect amid the applause,
As Turnus's indignant spirit sought the shades
And he lightheadedly pulled his sword from the corpse,
That he too was done for, the epic at an end?
For half his life it had served as his hiding-place,
A factitious destiny he'd gladly shouldered
Like a suit of armour, shielded within his role.
Who was he? No one had ever needed to ask.
He was pious Aeneas, heavily engaged
In the business of piety, and if that made
For a certain blankness, well what could you expect?
He felt his age now. Even the long-counted-on
Desire to cut loose was weaker than he'd supposed.
Yet, loitering facelessly about the palace,
He recalled certain landfalls with crushing regret,
The time at Carthage (that time in the stormlit cave),
And not Dido only but other instances
Too slight for the record, the curve of a veiled hip,
A smile out of shadow, a path leading away
Under palms or pines, dusty inconsequent track
To the untried life beyond omen or taboo...
Meanwhile he had become an encumbrance merely,
Ineffectual, daydream-sodden, a figurehead
Lolling aphasic, as life went on despite him
– Since there was a country to govern, after all;
(The past must not be allowed to get in the way).
Fidus Achates came to an understanding
With Queen Lavinia, who had motives of her own.

They smothered him with a pillow as he lay drunk
And dropped his body, weighed with stones, in the Tiber,
Then put out their story of apotheosis
And called in another poet, more biddable
Than the previous one, to fake up a thirteenth book.

Middle-Aged Query

Do we grow into, or out of, our hang-ups,
poetic, sexual?
            Or have we, simply,
become more easy about admitting them
and not minding it if another should mind –

unless by good fortune the minder happens
to share the hang-up?
            Then, O happy meeting!

Paysage Moralisé

A field become a torrent-bed! In vain
You look for any richness in this land.

The once-good soil is leached to the last grain.
You only stumble over reefs of sand.

Portrait of a Virtuoso

Coins, potsherds, fossils: always need and hope of
Discovery, design in little.
                              Looking
Was a half-life; finding meant full existence
(But that existence self-enclosed, unspoken,
One secret more among the household secrets)
For the timid virtuoso, twelve years old,
Who stares out searchingly from the photograph.

He has a claim upon me, and within me,
Which I can neither answer nor put aside.
Who is reaching to whom for what kind of help
Which can't be offered?
                              Yet there is common ground
On which to meet: the talismanic value
Assigned to certain objects, recollected
As vividly as if they lay in my palm,
Or I were standing beside that appletree,
Now long cut down, a hand on its scaly bark...

Curled *Gryphaea*, the lesser valve still intact,
Hinged in concave embrace to the outer shell,
'The Devil's Toenail'; an orange aurochs-tooth,
Broken-rooted, from Tertiary gravel;
Struck from its clayey nodule, an ammonite –
The ribbed circuits and mossy-patterned sutures
Of the shallow vortex perfectly exposed;
A flint scraper; a polished basalt axehead;
The black rim of a Tuscan pitcher, printed
With shapely roundels; an earthenware loom-weight;
An *as* of Vespasian, the patina'd face
Pitted by volcanic ash; a charred fragment
Of planking from a Roman galley:
                              items
From his cabinet of curiosities;
Each trophy labelled and set out on display,
A sop to reticence, an oblique challenge,
A wooing of the wide world of time and place.

No wonder that, despite his uncertain gift,
Poetry should have set an ambush for him
At the next turning.
                        What was it ran beneath
Such mixed anxiety and expectation,
If not compulsive longing for an enforced
Openness, by which things might be named and shown?

By the Loire

1

Grey heron –
Its shadow in the water
More visible than itself.

2

A kingfisher
– Or a torn scrap
Of turquoise litter
Snagged on a branch?

3

Ragged phoenix –
The cormorant, wings held open,
On its stone-island.

7

Virgil
The Georgics

Georgic 1

What livens the fields, at the prompting of what star
The earth should be turned and vines be joined to elms,
The breeding of sheep and cattle, the care of the herd,
And how to profit by the sweet reserve of bees,
These are my themes, Maecenas. Clear lights of heaven,
You stars that draw the seasons across the sky;
Bacchus and kindly Ceres, you by whose grace
The earth exchanged Dodona's acorns for bread
And mixed plain water with the juice of the grape;
You Fauns and Dryads who fill the woods and fields
With your living presence, come close and bless my poem:
I make it of your gifts. You, ranger of the hills,
Whose milk-white cattle browse on the thickets of Cea;
You, Neptune, for whom earth opened at a trident stroke
And the whinnying horse leapt into being, come close.
Great Pan, protector of the shepherd and the flock,
Now leave the coombs of Lycaeus, your ancient home,
To wait on my poem; and you, boy-lord of the plough;
Minerva, inventor of the olive tree; old Sylvanus,
The cypress sapling uprooted in your careful hand;
You gods and goddesses who watch over the fields;
Who have in your care the fruits that spring up unsown
And send down rain to water the planted crops.
And you, who must soon be counted among the gods,
By which of your powers, Caesar, are you to be known?
Shall willing nations be gathered beneath your sway
And the wide world welcome you as Lord of the Harvest,
Your forehead wreathed with myrtle, your mother's crown?
Will you come to us as god of the boundless sea,
The sailor's deity, distant Thule your servant?
Shall Tethys court you for son with a dowry of waves?
Shall a new star rise across the summer sky
Where the Scorpion pulls in his arms to make a space
In the Zodiac's arc, and the grieving maid withdraws?
In whatever shape of power you choose to come,
(Yet Tartarus shall never have you for its king
Nor your ambition be touched by so dark a wish,
Though Greece is lost in longing for Elysian Fields
And Proserpine forgets her mother and her home),
Sanction my bold adventure, since you share my pity

For the countryman ignorant of the land he works.
We need your presence. Be faithful to our need.

In early spring when snow melts away on the hills
And the soil softens at the touch of the west wind,
Let your bulls begin to groan as the plough cuts deep
And the share be worn by the furrow so that it shines.
The land which answers the farmer's jealous hopes
Must lie exposed twice over to sun and frost:
At last the gathered harvest will burst the barns.
But before you set the plough to unbroken ground
Take trouble to find out the nature of the place,
Its quirks of wind and weather, its well-tried ways,
Since each spot differs in what it bears or rejects.
One spot suits corn, another grapes, yet another
Plantations of trees and grass that needs no planting.
To India we look for ivory, to soft Sabaea
For frankincense, to Epirus for champion mares,
To Pontus for beaver's gall, to Tmolus for saffron,
To the Calybes, naked at the forge, for steel.
This is the law that nature has laid from the first
On certain places. The contract stands unchanged
Since Deucalion threw stones into the empty world
And men rose up and entered on their hard lives.
To work then! Where the soil is rich, start ploughing
In the first months of the year; let dusty summer
Bake the stiff-backed clods with its fierce beams
Or grass and weeds will hinder the growing crop.
Where the soil is poor, wait till Arcturus rises,
Then turn it up lightly with a shallow furrow:
Though loose and sandy, it will keep the moisture it has.

Every second year your land should lie fallow.
Let the fields grow rough and hard from lack of use,
Or else, as the seasons shift, plant other crops:
Where vetch or bitter lupin or quivering beans
Possessed the ground – a delicate undergrowth
Of rustling stalks – sow yellow corn instead.
A crop of oats or flax or somnolent poppies,
Unvaried from year to year, burns up the earth;
But grown alternately, they will do no harm
If you cover the parched acres with fattening dung
And scatter ashes across the exhausted soil.

For the fields also, a change is as good as a rest
And better than no return from unploughed land.

It is often helpful to fire the empty fields.
The tall stubble goes up in a splutter of flames.
Perhaps this strengthens the earth and makes it rich
With some hidden nourishment, or perhaps the burning
Gets rid of rottenness and superfluous damp.
Perhaps heat loosens the soil, opening the pores
So that sap can find its way into the new grass,
Or hardens it to resist extremes of weather,
Sealing the ground against thin constant rain
Or piercing frost or the heat of the rapid sun.
Once ploughing has broken the earth into heavy clods
Work it with mattock and wicker harrow. Let Ceres
Look down from Olympus, tumbling her yellow hair.
Or turn your plough against the stiff-backed ridges,
Driving it crosswise over the furrowed ground.
Take command of the fields and set them to work.

A farmer prays for wet summers and mild winters.
After a dusty summer the corn grows strongest:
Then wealthy Mysia boasts her richest harvests
And Gargarus marvels as the slopes embrown.
He does not count on the weather. The seed once sown,
He rushes the mounded ramparts, beats them down,
And channels water to freshen the sandy soil.
As scorching heat starts to wither the young crop
He diverts the stream where it runs above his fields;
It leaps with a throaty rush down the dried-out course
And spreads in gentle wellings, cooling the earth.
To keep the grain from growing too heavy for the stalk
He thins its richness by grazing early in the year,
Before the blade tops the furrow. Any marshy patch
He drains by sinking a trench of sand and gravel;
Especially where, in unsettled months, a torrent
Pours down, covering a stretch of ground with mud
And leaving shallow pools to fester in the sun.

But the labour of men and oxen in turning the earth
Is only part of the task. You must reckon the damage
That birds can do, the crane and gluttonous goose,
Tough-rooted weeds, thick shade. The first rule in farming

Is that you are never to hope for an easy way.
The land demands your effort: body and mind
Are sharpened, that untried would grow vague with sloth.
Before Jupiter's reign the fields had no masters.
Even to mark out land and divide it with bounds
Was unlawful. No one took thought of yours or mine
While the generous earth gave enough for every need.
Jupiter first put the poison in black snakes,
Sent wolves marauding, set the calm sea heaving,
Shook honey off the leaves, took fire away,
And stopped the wine that ran everywhere in streams:
So that men by slow experience should learn the skills
By which they live, plant furrows, wait for corn
And strike from flint the fire hidden in its veins.
Boats of hollowed alder were launched on the rivers.
Sailors numbered the stars and gave them names,
Pleiads, Hyads, Arctos, Lycaon's bright daughter.
Now men discovered how to surround steep coombs
With hunting dogs, to trap animals, to lime birds,
To lash the streams' deep pools with casting nets
And to haul their heavy tackle through the sea;
Tempered iron and the saw's shrill blade were used
Where before wood fell apart to a tap on a wedge;
And one by one the laborious skills were mastered
By which we shape the world to our own ends.
Ceres taught men to turn the earth with a plough.
In the grove at Dodona acorns and arbutus failed:
The old diet and old haunts were no longer enough;
The pain of a blighted harvest had still to be learnt.
Soon mildew attacked the corn, eating at stalks;
Tares bristled in the unkempt fields; a prickly growth
Of burrs and caltrops sprang up as the crops died;
Wild oats and thistles stood thick above the grain.
Then keep weeds down with your mattock, scare the birds
With shouts, thin out the shade cast by your trees
With a sharp billhook, call down rain with your prayers;
Or be ready to suffer the sight of your neighbour's harvest
And look in the woods under shaken oaks for your own.

I will speak now of the weapons used in this war,
Without which crops could neither be sown nor raised:
First the share and the curved plough's heavy timber
And the slow wagons that bring the harvest home;

Then weighty mattocks, sledges and drags for threshing,
And wooden hurdles; the common wicker baskets
Of Demeter's priest, the winnowing fan of Iacchus.
You must have all these in store and ready for use
If country honours are ever to be yours by right.
Search in the woods for an elm that has grown crooked,
Its trunk forced into the ploughstock's bending shape.
To this a pole should be fastened, eight foot long;
Beneath, two boards and a double ridge of share-beams.
Use linden for the yoke, since it weighs lightly,
Beech for the handle to guide and turn the plough;
Hang the wood over your hearth for smoke to season.

I can pass on to you many ancient maxims
If your attention admits such modest cares.
The threshing floor must be levelled with a heavy roller,
Dug over, and the surface packed hard with clay
To keep back grass and stop its cracking and crumbling.
Various pests will make inroads. The tiny mouse
Will set up his home and his granary underground;
The blind mole will move into digs at your expense.
The earth's recesses swarm with vermin; toads
Squat in dank hollows; weevils and scurrying ants,
Putting by for old age, ravage great heaps of corn.
When the walnut breaks into flower among the woods
And catkins with their strong scent hang along its branches,
Look closely: if most of the blossoms come to fruit
You can hope for a sweltering summer, a busy harvest;
But if the foliage is only rich in shade
Then chaff and straw will mock the thresher's labour.
I have often seen men drench seeds before sowing
With carbonate of soda and the black lees of oil,
To give substance to the bean-pod's promise – a crop
Which swells and softens, boiled on a gentle fire.
I have seen how seeds sorted with the utmost care
Will degenerate, unless every year the task
Of picking out the largest, one by one, is repeated.
Everything tends to the worse, if left to itself;
The current tugs; and the man straining at the oars
To hold his craft, to make a little headway
Is swept downstream if he rests his arms for a moment.

Bound to the land, we must keep as careful an eye

On the stars, Arcturus, the Kids, and the bright Dragon,
As sailors who work their way homeward across high seas
From stormy Pontus and the oyster-bearing straits.
When Libra balances the hours of night and day
And the world lies half in light and half in shadow,
Set your bulls ploughing, sow the fields with barley
Till the weather breaks and drives you from your work.
Now too is the time for planting flax and poppy;
So long as your ground is workable, lean at the plough
Though heavily laden clouds lie low in the sky.
Spring is the season for sowing beans and millet,
And the soil, left fallow, lies ready for lucerne.
The bright Bull opens the year; his horns are gilded
In triumph, and the Dog backs away as he comes on.
But if you work the ground for a harvest of wheat
Or hardy spelt, and your whole concern is for grain,
Wait till the Pleiads hide themselves in the morning
And the Cretan Girl has lost her burning crown
Before you commit to the furrow its due of seed
Or trust too early the hope earth cannot share.
Many begin before Maia's setting, but the harvest
Turns to wild oats from lying too long in the soil.
If you choose to sow kidney beans or Egyptian lentils
Or vetch, and do not despise such homely crops,
Then take the Bear-Keeper's setting as a sure sign:
Start sowing and continue till frosts grow sharp.

To mark the seasons the sun divides his journey,
Stage by stage, through heaven's twelve constellations.
Five zones make up the sky; a tropic zone
That flushes and quivers in the heat of the sun;
Round this, at either extreme, extends a region
Locked in blue cliffs of ice and dark with storms,
But the temperate zones – else we should not survive –
Are ours by divine gift, and through them runs
A slanted path where the signs of the Zodiac turn.
Heaven rises northward over the Scythian hills
And falls away, sloping to Libya and the south.
One pole stands high above us; the other lies hidden
Beneath our feet, with dark Styx and the Shades.
In our sky the Dragon twists and winds his coils
Like a river between the Great and Lesser Bear –
Stars scared to plunge in Ocean, that will not set.

But there, some believe, one season dark and silent
Holds the sky; night's shadow never thins;
Or else the dawn returns from us, bringing light,
And the breath of the sun's horses, our morning breeze,
Means dusk there and the kindling of the evening star.
Skies shift and weathers change. What the stars teach
Is a pattern in the change: when to sow and to reap,
When to strike with oars the sea's delusive glitter,
When to launch and rig the ships laid-up for winter,
When to fell the forest pine that frames the ships.
We are wise to know these signs, their setting and rising,
And the balance of seasons through the varied year.

When rain keeps him indoors, the farmer has time
For the odd jobs which would have to be done in a hurry
If the weather were clear. He hammers out the point
Of a blunted ploughshare or hollows wooden troughs
Or marks his cattle or sorts his sacks of grain.
He sharpens stakes and forked props, and prepares
Thin willow twigs to fasten and train his vines.
This is the time for weaving baskets from briars,
For grinding corn and drying it over the hearth.
There are jobs that can be properly undertaken
Even on festival days. No scruple forbids you
To water your fields or mend a broken hedge.
You can fire the brambles or set snares for birds
Or dip your loud flock in clear-running water.
On these days also a farmer goes to market
Loading his slow donkey with oil or apples,
And brings back a ridged millstone or lump of pitch.

There are certain days, determined by the moon,
Which help or hinder work. Watch out for the fifth:
Pale Orcus and the Furies were born that day
And monstrous Typhon and the giant sons of Earth
Who swore that heaven should be broken by their hate.
Three times they tried to pile Ossa on Pelion,
Then heave Olympus with its woods up Ossa's side –
Three thunderbolts from Jupiter levelled their work.
The seventeenth day is lucky for planting vines,
For taming oxen or setting a web in the loom.
The ninth is good for runaways, bad for thieves.

Some work is better done in the cool of night
Or early in the morning when the dew is shot with beams.
You should cut light stubble and mow your hayfields then,
Since at night the moist air softens the dry stalks.
One man I think of especially, who stays up late
Cutting torches with his knife by winter firelight,
While his wife sings as she works to the sharp accompaniment
Of the shuttle running to and fro across the web,
Or boils down sugary must to make a syrup,
Skimming the foam with leaves from the trembling cauldron.
But sunburnt Ceres goes reaping in the heat of the day,
In the heat of the day the roasted corn is threshed.
Strip off to plough and to sow. The farmers' slack time
Is winter; then they relish what they have struggled for,
Sharing each others' company and food and cheer,
Easy in themselves while the season entertains them –
Like sailors when their laden ships have come in
And they garland prows in the happiness of return.
Still there is work to be done, gathering of acorns
And olives, berries of the bay-tree and blood-red myrtle;
It is time to set snares for cranes and nets for deer,
To course the sharp-eared hare, bring down the roebuck
With hempen whirrings of the Balearic sling,
While snow lies deep and rivers chivvy their ice.

What need I say of the dangers which autumn brings?
You can read storms in the stars when days draw in
And the heat grows mild; or when spring pours down its showers
As the bearded harvest bristles in the fields
And grain swells full and milky on the green stems.
When the farmer has already set his reapers to work
Stripping the barley ears from the brittle stalks,
I have seen winds swoop down from a darkened sky
And wrestle each other over the yellow fields,
The harvest torn up and scattered to the air,
Straw and stubble swept off by the swirling gusts.
Often a gathering rainstorm towers overhead;
Clouds heap up, black with showers, closing in
The murky air, till the sagging sky bursts open
And all the labour spent in ploughing and sowing
Is washed away. Ditches fill. The hollow riverbeds

Rise roaring. The sea breathes hard about the coasts.
From a night of thunderclouds Jupiter hurls bolts.
His right hand gleams. The earth shakes far and wide
As the blow falls. Wild animals run for cover,
Men feel their hearts grow small with terror. The God
Strikes Athos or Rhodope or steep Ceraunia
At will. The wind redoubles, the rain falls sheer,
The forests and shores moan, beaten by the gale.
Be afraid of this as the months change with the stars.
Watch where the frozen planet of Saturn withdraws
And where Mercury wanders in his fiery orbit.
But first of all worship the gods and offer to Ceres
Her sacrifice, spilling blood on the new grass
At winter's end in the first fine days of the year.
Then lambs are fat and wines are at their smoothest,
Sleep beckons and the hills are heavy with shade.
Let the young men, the country round, honour Ceres.
Melt honeycomb into milk and soft wine for her.
Let the willing victim be led three times round the crops
Followed by a crowd, with cheers and shouts to Ceres
To get her attention and call her into their homes.
Before reapers set their sickles to the ripe ears
They must wreath their heads with oak leaves, sing and dance,
So that Ceres has her worship, honest and uncouth.

There are signs, ordained by God, from which we learn
What the weather will be, cold wind or rain or sun.
There are warnings, clear to read, in the moon's changes,
A sign for the south wind's slackening, tokens which tell
The farmer to move his cattle nearer their stalls.
At the wind's rising the sea lifts restlessly,
Fretting in its channels. A dry roaring is heard
Through the tall hills. The long whisper of the shoreline
Grows muddled, disturbed. The forest murmur thickens.
Waves knock at the curved timbers of ships' hulls
As if demanding entrance. Gulls swoop shoreward
Crying as they come, and ragged-winged cormorants play
Across dry land. The heron abandons the marshes
Where he kept watch and flaps high above the clouds.
When the wind is mounting, shooting stars are seen:
Their headlong glide whitens against the darkness,
A trail of flame drawn slow and brief through night.
Chaff stirs and falling leaves dance on the air.

On the water's surface small feathers scud and skim.
When thunder and lightning trouble the whole sky
The ditches run full, the country is set awash
And out at sea all hands take down drenched canvas.
Yet no one need ever be caught out by rain.
When a shower threatens, cranes leave off their flight,
Take cover in valley bottoms; cows look skyward
Spreading their nostrils, sniffing the air as it stirs.
Sharp flights of swallows scatter across still water.
Frogs rasp their harsh old singsong from the mud.
Ants wear a narrow path as they carry their eggs
From hidden store-rooms. A rainbow bends to drink.
Rooks rise from their foraging in disorderly troops,
Crowding the air, clapping their tattered wings.
Sea-birds and marsh-birds that flock in the Asian meadow
Picking about the pools of Cayster for food
Dabble their feathers, toss spray over their backs,
Or dash their heads in water and run at the waves,
Giving themselves to aimless joy as they bathe.
The raven announces rain with tactless cries
And struts in stately solitude along the beach.
Young girls, as they sit up spinning late at night,
Can tell that a storm is in the air when the oil
Sputters in the lamp and grows a scurfy crust.

Equally, there are signs which promise fair weather,
Clear sky and open sun after days of rain.
The blunted points of stars take a keener edge,
The light of the moon as she rises seems her own.
Thin shreds of cloud no longer trail through the sky.
Halcyons, the birds of Thetis, leave the shore
Where they opened their wings to the pale sun. Restless pigs
Stop tossing their filthy litter with their snouts.
Now fields and hollows fill with low-lying cloud;
The night-owl, watching sunset from his high perch,
Denounces the change with unrelenting calls.
Far up through the clear air Nisus floats into view:
Scylla must pay for her theft of the purple lock.
Wherever she feints and flutters as she flies
The hateful shadow of Nisus falls across her;
His wingbeat shakes the air. Wherever he shifts
She feints and flutters, starting away in flight.
Now rooks caw gently, three or four times over,

Through half-closed throats, debating with each other
In their lodges high among the leaves, subdued
By a strange well-being. They love it when rain has cleared
And they come back to their young in the ragged nest.
Their insight is neither God's nor nature's gift –
They have no special knowledge of things to be.
But when bad weather shifts and wet sky brightens
And a south wind drives the clouds in vast procession,
Gathering and settling, lifting and moving on,
The animals feel a corresponding change;
They look out at the world through freshened eyes.
This is what it means when birds break into song
And cattle frisk and rooks call throaty assent.

If you watch the spinning sun and changing moon,
Tomorrow's weather will never give you surprise
And the night, for all its stars, will not deceive you.
If the moon, as she gathers her returning fires,
Shows blurred from horn to horn through the dark air,
Then farmers and sailors must watch for heavy rain.
If a gentle blush spreads over her downcast face
And reddens its pale gold, winds are sure to rise.
If on the fourth day her look is bright and clear
And she crosses the night sky with horns unblunted,
You will know for certain that all the days to come
Till the month's end will be free of rain and wind –
Sailors, safe on shore, will discharge their vows
To Glaucus, Panopaea, and Ino's son, Melicerta.
The sun gives weather-signs also, both at his rising
And when he sinks in the waves: observed in the morning
Or when the stars come up, they are equally sure.
If he lifts above the horizon chequered with spots
Or scarfed in cloud, or dwindles to a hollow disc,
Be ready for wet gales blowing in from the sea –
A south wind harmful to trees and crops and flocks.
If at dawn the cloudy sky is shot with beams
Of splintered light; if Aurora leaves Tithonus
On a couch of yellow mist and rises pale,
What shelter can vineleaves give the ripening grapes
When dancing hailstones rattle loud on the roofs?
Remember to watch the sun when he hangs low
In the western sky. At his setting we often see
The colours change and wander across his face.

Blue means rain, a flamy colour wind.
But if dark spots are caught in his fiery gold
Expect vile weather, a night of rushing wind
And cloud, when only a fool would put to sea –
Let boats strain at their moorings along the shore.
But if his face shows clearly at the beginning
And end of his journey, there is no danger of rain:
A dry north wind will be stirring in the trees.
However the day turns out, fair weather or foul,
Rainless cloud or a storm brewing in the south,
The sun will tell you. Who calls the sun a liar?
He warns us of tumults, treacheries and wars,
The trouble festering beneath the surface of things.
Witness his pity for Rome when Caesar died
And he hid his face in a cowl of rusty cloud.
We dreaded that the light would never come back.
All nature was ominous then, earth, sea and sky:
Dogs barked our doom, birds shrieked it from the air.
Time after time the Cyclopses' furnaces burst:
We saw walls of lava slide down over the fields
And Etna's sides scattered with glowing coals.
A noise of battle hurtled through the German sky
And the Alps shook with tremors unfelt till then.
Breaking the stillness of sacred groves, a voice
Spoke suddenly out of all the air. Ghosts shimmered
At nightfall. Cattle were cursed with human speech.
Earth retched as its waters dried. The temple images,
Ivory and bronze, wept tears and ran with sweat.
Eridanus, the river lord of my home ground,
Tore up forests in his anger, drowned our fields,
Swept off cattle with their stalls. In that dark time
The entrails spelt a message threaded with pain.
Blood sprang from wells; towns, huddled on their hilltops,
Heard night echo with the ululation of wolves.
No days matched these: the clear sky shook with thunder;
Meteors, never so many, blazed their portents.
But the end, the struggle at Philippi, was as before –
Identical armies bent on each other's slaughter;
The broad plain of Haemus glutted a second time
With Roman blood while calmly the gods looked on.
In time to come, perhaps, as the farmer labours
Over those acres and his plough turns back the soil
He will uncover spearheads eaten by flaky rust

Or strike his heavy mattock against empty helmets
And gape at the great bones in their shallow graves.
Gods and Heroes of our country, Romulus, Vesta,
Guardians of Tuscan Tiber and the Palatine Hill,
Do not baulk this young man, hope of our fallen age,
As he labours to bring us clear of ancient harm.
Laomedon's debt was paid long ago with our blood.
But the court of heaven grows jealous of your presence among us,
Jealous of your triumph, Caesar, and wishes you home.
What place have you here amid the wreckage of wars
Where evil has plundered a sanction for every crime:
The pruning hooks beaten into swords, the plough
Dishonoured, the empty fields running to waste?
War stirs in Germany, stirs along the Euphrates;
Our cities quarrel, break pledges and rush to arms.
A savage Mars makes the world his stamping ground.
I think of how chariot teams pour out of their cages:
The pace increases; reins are useless; the horses
Run away with the driver; the car hurtles out of control.

Georgic 2

The fields have been tilled, the seasons marked by their stars.
The theme is yours now, Bacchus: quick-growing vines,
Slow olives, rich in harvest, and trees of the woods.
Let my poem be your vineyard, Lenaean father.
Grapes weigh the autumn land, the pressed juice foams,
The tubs stand brimming. All that is here is yours.
Be present, Lenaean father; join in the treading,
Pull off your boots, stain your bare legs with must.

The rearing of trees varies according to their kind.
Some come up by themselves without human prompting:
The soft osier, the slender broom, the poplar,
The willow with its grey leaves flashing white. To these
The fields and curving riverbanks belong for miles.
Some spring from seed, the chestnut and Jupiter's tree
The winter oak, thick-leaved, the tallest in the forest,
And the common oak, the oracle tree of the Greeks.
Others, like the cherry and elm, send up an undergrowth
Of dense suckers from their roots; the Parnassian bay-tree
Starts, a tiny shoot, in its mother's great shadow.
So nature shifts for herself, and trees of all species
Flourish in woodland, orchard, sacred grove.

Experience has taught that there are other ways also.
One man takes cuttings from the mother plant's tender stalk
And beds them in rows; another stakes his ground
With tougher stems, cut crossways or pointed for rooting.
Some trees must have their shoots pegged down as layers,
Quickset in the earth about them and bent like bows.
Others strike root however the cutting is taken;
Their topmost prunings can safely be set in the earth.
A seasoned piece of olive-wood, cut from the trunk,
Nothing, as it seems, more dead, will push out a root.
The branches of one tree change into those of another
By harmless grafting; so apples weigh the peartree,
Plums redden among the leaves of the stony cornel.

The way of tending each kind of tree must be learnt;
A farmer should have at his fingertips the skill
Of sweetening what is wild. No ground should lie idle. Let Ismarus

Be planted with vines, Tabernus be clothed with olives.
Join me in the task, Maecenas. I owe to you
The better part of my reputation and pride.
The sea where I spread sail opens vast before me.
I will not try to draw everything into my verses,
And could not, if I had a hundred tongues in my head
And a voice of iron. But the coastline is ours to follow,
The land shows clearly. Then trust me to avoid
Poetic fiction, its riddles, its long preambles.

Those trees which raise themselves up into the day
Unprompted, though barren, grow flourishing and strong,
Sustained by the soil's power. But if they are grafted
Or moved and planted out into well-dug trenches,
They shed their woodland nature, and tended with care,
Will readily follow the guidance that you give.
The same is true when a sucker that shoots up barren,
Close to the mainstem, is planted out in the open
Where the overbearing shadow of the mother tree
Can no longer reach to sap its power of growth.
A self-sown seedling takes time to get established.
It may yield your grandchildren a fine crop of shade,
But the fruit is poor and tasteless; the truant vine
Will hang its wretched bunches for birds to peck at.

There is never an easy way. The trees must be bedded
In trenches, one by one, and tamed by your effort.
Olives succeed best if they are grown from stakes,
Paphian myrtle from stems and vines from layers.
The tough hazel, the spreading ash, the poplar –
The tree of Hercules with its shady crown –
And the oak which fed our fathers, all grow from suckers;
So too the tall palmtree and the sea-destined pine.
The walnut may be grafted on the rough-barked arbutus;
Barren planes can be made to bear fine apples,
And beechtrees chestnuts; blossom of the pear has whitened
On the wild ash; pigs have chewed acorns under elms.

The methods of grafting and budding are not the same.
Where the tips of buds push out from beneath the bark
And burst their delicate sheaths, a notch is cut
Across the swelling and a sprout from another tree
Implanted there to grow into the sappy rind.

If the trunk is unknotty, the wood should be cut open
And a gap split deep by wedges for fruitful slips
To be put in. Before long, a vigorous tree
Will be spreading new branches to the sky and wondering,
As it flourishes, how it came by such leaves, such fruit.

Trees of a kind may vary. The strong elm, the willow,
The lotus, the cypress of Ida, come in different strains.
There are several sorts of olive, all rich in yield,
Each distinct in its leaf, its fruit and its oil.
King Alcinous' orchard has many kinds of apple.
One shoot never gave Crustumian and Syrian pears.
The grapes which cluster on our vines are not the same
As Lesbos gathers from her Methymnian stocks.
Vines of Thasos do best in a heavy soil,
Vines with white grapes from Marea prefer a light one.
There are Psithian raisin-wine, and light-bodied Lagean
To blur your speech and send you swimming home;
The Rhaetic, the Purple, the Precian, which has the prize?
But a taste of Falernian silences all debate.
Aminean vineyards yield the best-bodied vintage
Which Tmolian and royal Phanaean might rise to toast;
While the lesser Argite vine is second to none
For its stream of juice, a flavour kept through the years.
Rhodian is pleasant when dishes are cleared away
And the drinking begins; so too plump grapes of Bumastus.
But vines are innumerable in their names and natures.
Who could wish to reduce the variety to number?
One might as well ask how many grains of sand
Stir and ripple in the wind of the Libyan desert,
Or try to master the sea by counting its waves
When a gale from the east beats down the struggling ships.

Not every kind of soil suits every tree.
Willows grow by water, alders on marshy ground;
The barren wild ash chooses a rocky cleft;
Yews flourish on a cold north slope, myrtle on a seashore;
Bacchus spreads his vineyards on the open hills.
To the world's end, wherever ground is tilled,
From Arabia to the land of the daubed Geloni,
Trees have their native places. Black ebony
Belongs to India, frankincense to Sabaea.
I think of the balsam-tree, its sweet-smelling wood,

Its oozings, of the podded acacia with gummy leaves,
Of cotton that whitens Ethiopian glades
And delicate silks that the Chinese comb from leaves;
I think of Indian forests near the final Ocean
Where the land curves back, bordered by trees so tall
That no man can shoot an arrow over their tops,
And yet that people are skilled in use of the bow.
Media produces the citron, with its bitter juice,
Its lingering taste: no remedy more effective
Against a jealous stepmother's cup of poison;
It stops the drug and heals the body from within.
The tree stands large and looks most like the bay;
You would mistake it if it were not for the scent.
Its blossom clings and its leaves withstand all winds.
The Medes use it in a rinse to sweeten their mouths
And give it to the old as a cure for breathlessness.

But Media with all its wealth of citron groves,
Ganges with its beauty, and Hermus fished for gold
Cannot contend with Italy; nor can Bactra nor India
Nor the Isle of Panchaea and its incense-bearing sands.
No flame-throwing bulls have ploughed these fields, no clutch
Of dragon's teeth been flung from the sower's hand
Nor crop of iron warriors bristled from the earth.
Ours is a plainer story: of vineyards and olive groves,
Of herds well-stocked, and harvests that will not fail.
Across our fields the war-horse proudly prances.
Here graze the snowy sheep and the great bull-victim
Which you, Clitumnus, bathe in your holy waters
To lead the Romans in triumph to shrines of the gods.
Here spring is importunate, summer will not leave us,
Our flocks bear twice, our orchards serve us twice;
We suffer no encroachment from lions and tigers;
Our gathered herbs are free from the aconite's poison;
The monstrous serpent which pours fold into fold
Or lifts on his scaly coils is not to be found here.
Think too of our cities, monuments, great works,
Our towns, so many, set high on their rocky cliffs
And the rivers gliding beneath their ancient walls;
Of the seas that wash our coastline, east and west;
Our great lakes, you, Larius first, and you, Benacus,
Whose billows break with the roaring of the sea.
Think of our harbours, how the waves chafe and seethe

At the Lucrine Pool's new-built defence; the waters
Of the Port of Julius hear them and remain calm;
The Tyrrhene Sea flows channelled into Avernus.
Our land is rich in metals; she opens veins
Of silver and copper; her rivers have turned up gold.
The men she rears are a fierce breed: Marsians, Sabines,
Ligurians, toughened by trouble, Volscian spearsmen,
The Decii, the Marii, great Camillus, the Scipios,
Unyielding captains, and last and greatest name,
Yours, Caesar, conqueror of Asia from coast to coast,
Fender of the poor Indian from the towers of Rome.
Country of Saturn, great mother of crops and men,
For you I speak of an ancient honourable livelihood;
Have traced my theme boldly to its hidden source
And fetched the song of Ascra through the towns of Rome.

I will deal now with the nature of different soils,
Their strength, their colour, the crops which grow best on each.
Where the ground is an awkward mix of gravel and clay
The long-lived olive will flourish; the grudging hillside
Disowns its thorns and softens at Athene's gift.
You can tell the soil by the oleaster rising thick
And the wild berries that it scatters underfoot.
But where the landscape opens in grassy levels,
Its soil benign yet clammy, made rich with ooze,
Or where a hammock low-slung from encircling hills
Catches the sift of earth which streams have washed down
From the bare ridges, or a southward facing slope,
Matted with roots of bracken, waylays the plough –
The ground will one day produce strong vines, a vintage
Running in streams, grapes that crowd to the hand,
Wine fit to be spilt in offering from a golden cup
When the plump Etruscan has blown his ivory pipe
By the altar and dishes are heaped with steaming bowels.
But if your concern is with animals, the rearing
Of calves or lambs, or goats that burn where they graze,
You should look for pasture as far as wealthy Tarentum
Or the plain of ravaged Mantua, lost to us now,
Where snowy swans browse on river-floated grass.
You have water for your herds and turf to feed them;
A cold dew on a summer night is enough there
To refresh meadows cropped through the long days.
A black soil that turns up rich beneath the plough

And crumbles naturally as the tiller works it
Is best for corn: no ground will send wagonloads
Rumbling home in such numbers, slowdrawn by oxen;
Or land where the frustrate labourer, clearing scrub,
Has levelled the casual growth of years of neglect,
Roots wrenched skyward, nesting places destroyed,
Birds scattered to the vast air, and furrow by furrow,
The unkempt acres ploughed to a gleaming sameness.
The loose uneven surface of shaly slopes
Offers no more than low spurge and rosemary for bees,
While flaky tufa, or chalk – black vipers eat it –
Boast that for snakes no food is better than theirs,
No ground so full of coiled recesses to hide in.
But soil which breathes out a thin soon-vanished mist
And drinks in moisture as it wants, or lets it go,
Which never changes greensward for other clothing
Or crusts iron tools with scurf or salty rust,
Is the one that weaves vines quickly about the elms
And bears fat olives, and as you will find by working it,
Is good for cattle and gently suffers the plough.
Rich Capua and the coast by Vesuvius know this,
And Clanius, flooding Acerrae's empty country.

Let me tell you how to recognize each of these kinds.
If you want to know whether a soil is loose or thick
– For Ceres and Bacchus differ in their chosen ground;
Corn likes a thick soil, the vine a very loose one –
Choose a place where the ground has lain undisturbed:
Sink a pit there, then fill it again with the earth
That has been removed and tread the surface well down.
A looser soil runs short: you will know it belongs
To cattle or vines. But if, when the pit has been filled,
There is still some left which refuses to go back,
Then the soil is thick and sluggish: you need strong oxen
To break it open and crumble the stiff-backed clods.
To learn if a stretch of ground is brackish or sour,
Useless for growing things, unresponsive to ploughing,
Thief of the vine's blue blood and the apple's good name,
This test will serve you: take down a wicker basket
Or a winestrainer from its place by the smoky roof;
Pack into it some of this bad earth mixed with water
Fresh from the spring; you will find when all the moisture
Strains out and falls in large drops through the twigs

That it carries the sharp flavour with it; proof of this
Can be read in the wry faces of those who taste it.
The simplest way of telling if a soil is rich
Is to work it in your fingers: instead of crumbling
It softens like pitch when held, and is sticky to touch.
How fiercely grass shoots up where the soil is moist!
Be on your guard. When ground is too ready to bear,
Too quick in its strength, then the corn will go to straw.
A close soil betrays itself silently by its weight,
A light one also; and the colour, pale or dark,
Can be told at a glance. But a cold delinquent soil
Is hard to discover, though these may give you warning:
Pitch-pines, black-berried ivy, damaging yews.

When you know your ground and have heaped trenches high,
Leave it as it is, the upturned clods exposed
To bake in the sun and freeze in the winter air,
Before you dig in your vines. A crumbling soil
Is the one you want, the effect of winds, fierce frosts
And the labourer swinging his mattock from dawn to dusk.
Some farmers, unwilling to spare any precaution,
Prepare a nursery for the rearing of cuttings
Much like the place that awaits them on transplanting
So that the slips should not think their mother changed.
They mark the stems, showing how each turns away
From the northern sky to face the heat of the south,
Then plant them out to stand as they stood before –
So deeply engrained are the habits learnt in youth.
You must know if a vine belongs to the fertile plain
Or the sparse hills. On rich low-lying soil
Plant close together, since a crowded vineyard thrives.
On rising ground and the broad backs of hills
Space out the rows, but at the same time make sure
That the avenues square exactly where they cross:
As a legion unfolds its long battalions in war
When the marching column has halted on open ground
And is marshalled in order, a flashing bronze tide
That sways and hovers with the War God's indecision
Before the deluge of battle sweeps the field.
Let the vineyard be measured and patterned, lane by lane,
Not merely to feed an empty passion for neatness,
But so that the earth will give equally of its strength
And branches have space around them to make their own.

You will ask to what depth the trenches should be dug.
The vine I would trust to a shallow furrow, but trees
Must be planted deep, belong far down in the earth,
Especially the oak: this reaches with its roots as close
Toward Tartarus as its branches open to the sky.
No winter storms will wrest it from its fixedness.
It endures, a living landmark, from age to age,
Burying the children that have played about its roots,
And stretches strong arms with sheltering unconcern
On every side to carry the burden of shade.

Never plant a vineyard to face the setting sun.
Never sow hazels among vines. Never take cuttings
From tender branch-ends or from high up on the tree:
What is close to earth loves earth. Never wound seedlings
With a blunted knife. Never graft the fertile olive
On the wild: if unthinking shepherds let fall a spark
It will fester slowly beneath the bark's rich cover,
Take hold of the trunk, slip upward, start with a crackle
High among the leaves and run from branch to branch,
From tree to tree, with fierce mastering ease
Till all the grove belongs to the whirling flames
And pitchy smoke-clouds billow blackly skyward,
But most when a storm has flung itself down on the woods
And a driving wind presses the fire before it.
The trees are betrayed by their roots, and once cut back,
Earth cannot help them to be as they were before.
The unblessed wild olive with its bitter leaf remains.

Pay no attention when busy neighbours warn you
That your vines should be planted out before winter's end.
What chance have the slips of taking hold in the soil
When the north wind blows and stiff frost seals the ground?
Spring is your season, when the white bird returns
And the long snake writhes in terror from its attack,
Or that time in early autumn when the weather still holds
But the year dwindles and the sun shines without warmth.
Spring is the trees' best time, they live for the spring.
Look how the soil swells, craving the lively seed,
How the fostering sky lets go his pent up rains
And body to body, with an enormous quickening,

Pierces the earth to nourish all that she bears.
Then pathless thickets are resonant with birdsong.
Animals return to coupling at their settled times.
Warm western winds stroke the soft bellies of the fields
And in everything sap rises with tender desire.
Plants lift more trustingly to the sun each day.
The sprouting vine, unafraid of southern gales
Or rain driven down by big winds from the north,
Pushes out buds and unfolds leaf by leaf.
It must have been like this at the world's beginning.
I think of that early time when things took shape
In their first integrity. It was original spring,
The whitening days unflawed by winter winds.
Then cattle first drank the light; the earthbound race
Of men rose up head foremost from stony fields;
Beasts were sent into the woods, stars into the sky.
Young plants could never carry through their task of growth
If there were not this respite between heat and cold
When the sky looks welcomingly on the newborn earth.

For the rest, wherever you plant your ground with cuttings,
Manure them lavishly, cover them well with earth
And bury rough shells or porous stones for drainage.
These let water through, give them room to breathe,
A chance to gather their strength. It is not uncommon
For a farmer to make a cover of rocks and potsherds,
A barricade to protect them from pelting rain
Or the Dog-star's heat when fields crack with thirst.

Once the slips are planted out, you must work the soil
Till it crumbles about the roots. Take a heavy mattock
To burst the clods, or turn the earth with a plough
And drive your labouring bullocks between the vinerows.
Prepare supports for the vines, smooth reed-stems, poles
Of shaven ashwood, strong forks to set beneath.
So steadied, they will learn to scorn the wind and climb
From tier to tier of branches high up through the elms.

When newly-fledged and in the first freshness of growth
The vines should be left alone. As they stretch in the breeze
And race with unhindered speed through the clear air
They are still too young for pruning; use your fingers
To thin them, nipping away redundant leaves.

But once they have spread and taken hold of the elms
And the stems have thickened, teach them to check their pride
And to know their master. Let the reproof be harsh:
Strip off the shoots, cut back the too-fast-growing sprays.

Hedges should be kept in repair to shut out stray animals,
But most when the vineshoots are young and untried by trouble.
The worst of storm and sun cannot cause such havoc
As casual inroads made by sheep and goats,
Forest-wandering buffalo or greedy heifers.
A frosty winter which freezes the ground solid,
Or a heavy summer, scorching the rocky heights,
Does harm. But not so much harm as the teeth of goats
Which leave a poisonous ulcer on the bitten stems.
For its crime the goat is slaughtered on Bacchus's altar
And satyr-songs are sung on the tragic stage.
The Children of Theseus offered the goat as a prize
For clownish games in villages and at crossways;
They played at balance-on-the-wineskin, drunk in the fields.
The farmers of Italy, true sons of Troy,
Sing bantering rounds in rough uproarious verse
And put on outlandish masks which they make of bark.
They fill their singing, Bacchus, with your shouted name
And hang little images of you in the tall pines:
Each vineyard grows up and swells with ripening fruit
And the hollow valleys fill in their long recesses
Wherever the flushed god shows his honest face.
So we honour Bacchus according to his rite
With homely hymns, bringing dishes of sacred cakes.
The he-goat stands at the altar, led by the horn.
We roast the rich meat in pieces on hazelwood spits.

But the dressing of vines demands yet further labour.
The task has no end. Three or four times a year
The ground should be dug over, clods broken up
With the back of a mattock, all the leafage thinned.
Task follows task for those who work the ground
And year tracks year in a never-broken round.
Once the vineyard has let go its last late leaves
And a cold north wind has broken the woods' pride,
The farmer, worried and eager, is already looking
To the coming year. He turns on the leafless vines
With Saturn's hook and prunes them back into shape.

Be first to dig the ground, first to burn up
The prunings, first to move the poles under cover.
Be last to gather. Twice leaf-shadow threatens the vines.
Twice thick weeds and briars overrun the vineyard.
Hard work is the only remedy. So give your praise
To a large estate; be content to farm a small one.
There are still rough broom-stalks to be cut in the woods,
Switches of untended willow, reeds from the river.
When the vines are tied and the hook can be put away,
And the vine-dresser bursts out singing, his last row done,
Still the earth must be chivvied and broken into dust;
The Sky God still has ripening grapes at his mercy.

Olive trees, by contrast, need little tending.
When once they have taken hold and faced the weather
They can do without curved hook or patient mattock.
The earth, by itself, gives moisture for a heavy crop
If the ploughshare loosens the ground and lays it open.
Do this at least for the sleek and peaceful olive.

Fruit-trees also, as soon as they find their strength
And feel the trunk firm beneath them, push out and upward
With inborn force. They have no need of our help.
Birds feast off blood-red berries in the unkempt thickets
And every tract of woodland grows heavy with fruit.
There is clover to cut, there are pines in the high forest
To feed our torch-flames and widely fling their light.
When so much is given, can men begrudge their labour?
Take the commonest plant and reckon its many uses,
How willow or lowly broom gives the browse of flocks,
The shepherd's shade, the fieldhedge, the food of bees.
Waving boxwood of Cytorus, pitch-pines of Naryx –
How it cheers the mind to see them! So with all landscapes
Where the harvest is innocent of human labour.
Even on the peaks of Caucasus, the barren forests
Which the east wind breaks and tears with lively fury
Are rich in kinds of timber, each with its use:
Cedar and cypress for houses, pinewood for ships,
Hard woods which are turned and cut to make spokes and wheels
For farmers' wagons, or laid as keels for boats.
Osiers come from the willow, leaf-fodder from the elm,
Spear-shafts from myrtle, and from the warrior's tree –
The cornel. Taut yew makes Iturean bows.

Smooth lime and boxwood, shiny from the lathe,
Take shape beneath the chisel and are hollowed out.
The boats that skim the rough surface of the Po
Are built of alder. The rotten holm-oak opens
And takes a swarm of bees to its hollow heart.
What blessings has Bacchus given to set beside these?
There is as much mischief as good in him. Drunken fury
Destroyed the Centaurs, Rhoetus, Pholus, Hylaeus –
Wielder of the winebowl to club the Lapiths down.

O farmers would be too happy if they did not live
In ignorance of their happiness. Far from the battlefield
They get their living from the even-handed earth.
No palace will open its tall gates for them,
No early visitors pour from the choked halls.
Doors set with tortoiseshell, garments shot with gold,
Bronzes from Corinth: they will never ogle these,
Never spoil the whiteness of wool with Assyrian dye
Nor, for scent, mix cinnamon with good olive oil.
Chance and anxiety have no hold on their life.
The wealth they count is the slow pace of the farm,
The secret freshness of rock-hollows, pools and coombs,
The lowing of oxen, sleep stretched out under trees,
Good hunting in the upland meadows and woods.
The young grow up uncomplaining, happy with little,
Respectful of gods and men. Here Justice lingered
Dragging her steps before she abandoned the earth.

One hope possesses me, that the gracious Muses
Accept the service of their passionate pilgrim,
That they teach me to understand the paths of the stars,
The sun's varying eclipses and the moon's labours;
What power it is that causes the earth to tremble,
The sea to swell, break bounds, and settle again;
Why the winter sun hurries so fast to bathe
In Ocean; what hindrance slows the tedious night.
But if the secrets of nature remain closed to me,
If the cold blood round my heart prevents such insight,
Let the fields, valleys, streams, rivers, woods
Make good my failure. O where the landscape opens –
Spercheus, Taygetus where Spartan girls meet their god,
The sheltered crannies of Haemus – O give me these,
Shield me with branches, let me be lost in the shade.

If the greatest happiness is that power of insight
Which enables a man to trample on his fear of death,
To accept the fact of it and discard the myth,
There is happiness too in the countryman's care of his gods,
Pan, old Sylvanus, and the sisterly Nymphs.
The rods of office, the favour of kings or crowds
Mean nothing to him, nor faction, nor brothers at odds;
Not the Danube oath that binds the Dacian horde
Nor Roman policies nor collapsing kingdoms.
Want cannot grieve him with pity nor wealth with envy.
What the fields and orchards willingly provide
He takes. Not for his eyes the iron laws,
The frenzy of the forum, the records of the state.
Others may trouble the blind sea with oars,
Rush against steel, break into the courts of kings.
A city may lie in ruins to bring one man
A bed of Sarran scarlet and a jewelled cup.
Some hide their wealth and brood on buried gold.
Some are knocked silly with rhetoric, some ravished
By the packed theatre's promiscuous acclaim.
Some take pleasure drenched in their brothers' blood,
Then wear out exile, searching for a land
That preserves the sweetness they destroyed at home.
But the farmer tills his patch, year in, year out,
With his crooked plough. His country, his family,
His cattle, his patient team – he supports all these.
And the year allows no interval. It overflows
With fruit, with sheaves of corn, with young for the herd.
It crowds the furrows with harvest, bursts the barns.
Winter comes: time to gather and press the olives.
Pigs leave their feast of acorns; the arbutus blooms.
Autumn has spread the table with all its fruits.
The vine has sweetened long since on its sunny cliff –
And his children climb about him to catch at kisses,
And his wife with homely modesty keeps house.
His cows let down full udders; his full-fed goats
Lock horns and jostle on a battlefield of grass.
On festival days you find him with his friends
Stretched on the earth round a fire with a demijohn of wine.
His prayer invites you, Bacchus. He sets up a target
On an elm for his herdsmen to try their skill in shooting,
Or they strip and wrestle, matching their tough limbs.
This is the life which the ancient Sabines lived once,

And Remus and his twin; this made Etruria strong.
From such beginnings Rome grew to all her splendour
And a city wall encompassed the seven hills.
In the age before the Dictaean king took power,
Before men broke faith and killed their oxen for meat,
Golden Saturn lived such a life here on earth.
The trumpet that calls to arms was still unblown,
The clatter of sword on anvil had never been heard.

But we have covered an immense distance in our course;
The horses steam in harness. It is time to release them.

Georgic 3

Great Pales, goddess of flocks, shepherd of Amphrysus,
Woods and streams of Lycaeus, my poem is yours now.
The stories which might serve to please careless minds
Have grown dull with use. Who needs to tell or be told
How Eurystheus raged or Busiris welcomed his guests,
How Leto gave birth or the boy Hylas drowned
Or Pelops of the ivory shoulder won his race
And his wife together? I must choose another path
To win ascendancy over the tongues of men.
If I live I will be the first to lead the Muses
Captive in triumph from the Aonian mountain,
The first, Mantua, to bring you Idumaean palms.
I will build a marble temple beside the water
Where Mincius winds his course in slow wide curves
Among green fields, and slender reeds edge the banks.
There Caesar shall preside, the god of the temple.
I will come to him, a conqueror dressed in scarlet;
In his honour chariot teams shall race by the river;
All Greece shall leave Alpheus and the groves of Nemea
To compete in the Games: quick foot and heavy glove.
I will crown my head with a garland of clipped olive
And bring him gifts. I can see now in my mind
The procession to the shrine, the oxen slaughtered,
The painted stage as it changes from scene to scene,
The inwoven Britons who lift the purple curtain.
On the doors I will set a battle in ivory and gold:
The people of the Ganges beaten by Roman arms,
The Nile swollen in battle and running high,
And columns of warships lifting bronze-shod prows,
The conquered cities of Asia, subdued Niphates,
The Parthian turning in flight to take sure aim,
The double foe defeated and trophy won
By the same hand, and conquests east and west.
Statues will stand there, shapes of breathing marble:
The children of Assaracus, Jupiter's descent,
Tros the founder, and Apollo the builder of Troy.
I will show the end of rebellion: tormenting Furies,
Hell's harsh river, the rock of Sisyphus,
Ixion bound by snakes to the racking wheel.
But now to the wooded hills and unkempt groves –

It is hard, Maecenas, the task you have given me;
Without your help there is no beginning. Come then,
We must hurry. On Cithaeron, on Taygetus, the hounds
Give tongue; Epidaurus, breaker of horses, calls us;
The folds of the hills echo with clamorous assent.
Later I will raise my verse to Caesar's wars
And spread his name in splendour as far through time
As time has elapsed since Tithonus was a child.

Whether a man breeds horses to win the palm
In racing, or sturdy bullocks for the plough,
He should choose the mother with care. The cow he wants
Has a lowering look, great head and brawny neck.
Her dewlap hangs from her chin down toward her thighs.
Her flanks are long; all parts large, even her feet,
And her ears are hairy beneath her crooked horns.
If her coat is patched with white, so much the better.
She baulks at the yoke and sometimes butts in anger,
Is more like a bull to look at, thickset and tall,
And sweeps her tracks with her tail as she walks.
The best age for mating and for bearing young
Begins at four years and ends before ten. The rest
Of their time they are unfit for breeding or ploughing.
But so long as the lively spirit of youth holds sway,
Let loose the males. Be early to give your cattle
The enjoyment of love; let each cow have her calf.
The best days are soonest past. Old age and sickness
Pull down all creatures from their defenceless prime
And time's encroachment only has one end.
There will always be some animals you need to change.
Replace these at once; look ahead, foresee your losses
And choose new stock each year to build up the herd.

The matter of choice applies no less to horses.
The animals you select to keep as stallions
Must be treated from the beginning with stricter care.
A young thoroughbred shows his nature at once
In the proud ease of his movement, his springy step.
He will lead the way, be the first that dares to cross
A dangerous stream or to trust an unknown bridge.
Empty noise will not scare him. His neck is upright,
His head is neat, his belly short, his back broad;
His breast flickers with muscle. Chestnut and grey

Are the best colours, white and dun the worst.
If he happens to hear the distant clash of arms,
He pricks his ears. His limbs tremble. He whinnies,
The red of his nostrils flares like furnace doors.
Tossed up, his mane falls thick over his right shoulder;
His back is furrowed where the spine runs; his hooves
Ring as if made of flint when he paws the ground.
So Cyllarus looked, the beast whom Pollux tamed
In Amylcae; such, the Grecian poets tell us,
The horses of Mars and the team of great Achilles;
So Saturn saved himself when, surprised by his wife,
He sprouted a horse's mane, neighed, galloped away;
High Pelion echoing his dread of being found out.

But as soon as a horse is touched by the reproach
Of age and disease, be ruthless. Shut him away.
Grown old, a stallion loses his taste for love
And his pleasure in labour. If ever he enters battle
His rage has no more strength than a stubble fire,
Fierce, ineffectual. So take account of his years
And his spirit first, of his other qualities after –
Pedigree, pride in winning, distaste for defeat.
Look how the chariot teams pour out of their cages,
Snatching at ground as the young drivers start forward
In breakneck rivalry. Hope and excitement empty
Their pounding hearts. They lean over slackened reins,
They ply their whips, till the axles burn with speed.
One moment you see them graze the ground, the next
Flung up through the air as if they had taken flight.
There can be no respite. The sand is thrown aside
In yellow showers; each would-be champion feels
Hot on his neck, his pursuers' foamy breath.
Erichthonius was first to join horses to a chariot
And stand in triumph as wheels carried him onward.
The Lapiths of Pelethron added reins, invented
The art of riding. They taught the horseman under arms
How to paw the ground, to curvet and proudly prance.
What the trainer needs for either purpose – and both
Are hard to attain – is a young horse, fast, full of mettle:
No matter if another is the veteran of many fields
Or claims Epirus or Mycenae for his country
Or traces back his descent to Neptune's original.

Once the animals are chosen and the time approaches
The breeder's concern is to fatten the one appointed
Chieftain and lord of the herd, to wait on him
With corn, with freshcut grass and freshdrawn water,
To give him strength for the pleasant exacting task –
Since a hungry father begets a puny child.
But the rest of the herd he purposely makes lean:
As soon as the stirring instinct sets them on edge
He keeps them short of food, drives them from water,
Shakes them with running and tires them in the sun.
The threshing floor groans under the tread of his mares
As a breeze from the west scatters the winnowed chaff.
He does this to prevent ease from silting their wombs
And dulling the keenness of the furrow to receive.
They starve, made greedy for the joy when it comes.

Now it is the turn of the mothers for special care.
The months pass. They wander loose in the fields.
They should not be yoked and set to draw heavy wagons
Nor forced to leap and jostle on the path, nor allowed
To run nor to struggle against fast-flowing water.
Leave them untasked to graze the forest meadows,
The borders of streams emerald with grass and moss,
To shelter by rock hollows and in the stretched shade of cliffs.
There is a kind of gadfly which breeds in swarms
In Sila's uplands and where green holm-oaks darken
The slopes of Alburnus – it is also known to the Greeks.
Its sting is fierce; the sound of its whizzing flight
Scatters the terrified herd and fills woods and sky
With bellowing along the dried-out course of Tanagrus.
Juno in her jealous anger once sent this creature
To torment Io the heifer-daughter of Inachus.
The hotter the day, the keener the gadfly's attack.
Avoid it, when your cows are in calf, by pasturing them
At sunrise, or when the stars bring on the night.

After the birth, the calves must have all your care.
Brand them to mark their parentage and the use
Assigned to each: set some aside for breeding,
Some for sacrifice, some to be put to the plough,
To break fallow ground and cast it up in clods.

Turn loose the other calves to graze as they will;
But begin at once the training of those you keep
To work the land; set them on the right road early
While youth still makes them amenable, ready to learn.
Bind a circlet of withy loose around their necks
And when they are used to this separate constraint,
Join them to one another by tying their collars,
Matching like to like, and make them walk in pairs.
First let them practise pulling unloaded wagons,
Their light tread scarcely marking the dusty ground,
Then weigh the beechen axle till it creaks and strains
As they haul the bronze shaft and the wheels ride forward.
You may feed them on grass and the willow's slender leaves
And marshy sedge, but while they are still unbroken
Gather corn in the blade for them. And do not repeat
Our fathers' mistake, and milk the nursing heifers.
Let the whole udderful go to those it was meant for.

But if your concern is for battle's fierce squadrons,
Or the racecourse: to drive your chariot where Alpheus glides
Past Jupiter's precinct, and to outpace its waters,
You must first train a horse to bear the sight of men armed
And ready for combat, to withstand the blast of trumpets,
The screech of wheels, the harness jangling in the stall;
Exerting himself more and more to win the praise
That he loves, and the soft commending slap on his neck.
Make him dare all this as soon as he is weaned.
Let his mouth yield sometimes to the novice's bit
Though he trembles in weakness, ignorance and youth.
But when three summers have passed and the fourth begins
Let him learn to pace a circle and order his steps
With a clean flowing movement and a ringing sound,
Till the task confines him. Then let him challenge the wind,
Gallop over open ground as if reins could not hold him,
His light hooves hardly scuffing the sandy earth:
As the north wind gathers and sweeps down from its quarter,
Driving Scythian storms and rainless clouds before it –
Then small gusts seethe through fields of standing corn,
Shiver the surface of waters, stir the treetops
To a louder whisper, and curl long waves against the shore:
Land or sea is all one to the blast when it strikes.
Such a horse will go all out for the winning post
Sweating circuit after circuit, mouth bloodied with foam,

Or will draw a fine carriage, delicately harnessed.
Once the breaking-in is done, let him eat coarse mash
To strengthen his ample body. If you give it him sooner
He will not be managed, and too spiritedly refuses
To obey the curling whip and the biting curb.

To maintain the strength of your animals, be careful
To guard them against the inward promptings of love.
Your cattle and your horses are equally at risk.
Let the bulls be sent off to graze deserted fields
On the further side of a river or ridge of hills
Or else shut up in their stalls with plenty to eat.
The sight of a heifer burns and melts their strength.
Her presence makes them forget the grass at their feet.
She stirs their rivalry as she stirs their lust,
And two will struggle to win her, horn locked to horn.
She grazes Sila's uplands, calm in her beauty,
While with charge and countercharge they fight it out,
The blood from many wounds darkening their sides.
Crashes are heard as they fling themselves together;
A furious bellowing fills woods and sky.
They cannot share a stable. One or the other
Must yield, broken in the fight, and withdraw far off,
Taking with him the injury and shame of defeat;
The love he has lost belongs to his proud conqueror;
One last look back and he goes like a banished king.
Through days and nights of exile, brooding his return,
He hardens himself with rough living, a bed of stones,
A diet of sharp-edged rushes and prickly leaves.
He learns how to make his horns declare his fury
And tests himself, butting treetrunks, slashing the air,
Pawing up ground as if battle had begun.
Once he has recovered strength he advances again:
He rushes his enemy, catching him off guard,
Like a wave which begins to whiten far out at sea,
Gathering behind it the lifted force of waters
As it curls shoreward and roars across the rocks,
A fluid mountain that tears itself from its base
To topple and break in eddies of black sand.

All living creatures are made distraught by lust.
Man, beast, bird, fish – no species is exempt.
Through water, earth and air the same fire runs.

Driven by lust, the lioness leaves her cubs
To wander in random fury across the plain;
The monstrous bear spreads carnage through the woods;
The boar and tigress rage; and the lonely traveller
Through Libyan desert takes fear by the hand.
Look how a stallion trembles in his whole body
If he catches the familiar taint on the breeze.
No reining-in nor angry whipping holds him,
No obstacle – rocky ridge or hollowed cliff
Or boulder-toppling river – stands in his way.
In Sabine hills the wild pig rushes, whets
His tusks, digs up the ground, rubs against trees
Back and forth, to proof his skin against wounds.
Remember the boy – love spilt its molten pain
Along his bones – who swam the stormy straits
At dead of night while the sky tumbled about him
And thunder crashed and the crag-torn sea roared out.
No care for grieving parents could withhold him,
No care for the girl whose life hung on his own.
Lust drives fierce wolves and dogs and spotted lynxes,
The creatures of Bacchus. It makes stags turn and fight.
But mares will surpass all these in wanton frenzy.
It was Venus who set them on in Potniae
When their savage jaws tore Glaucus limb from limb.
They climb the mountain ridges, swim the rivers.
Past Gargarus, Ascanius, passion leads them on;
And as soon as the flame has got into their bones
– When spring comes back and their bodies feel the heat –
They stand on high crags, facing into the breeze
That blows from the west; till – strange but true – it happens
That the wind impregnates them with no stallion by.
Then they break away, bounding across the rocks
And down where the land unfolds in long coombs
That slope seaward; never running to the east,
But north or where black gusts freeze the southern sky.
But what is the issue of this elemental coupling?
A poisonous juice distilling in their groins
Which shepherds call horse-frenzy, and stepmothers use
To beat with herbs while chanting magic spells.

But time slips by, slips by and cannot be reclaimed
While we dwell on details and affection waylays us.
Enough now of cows and horses. A further part

Of our subject remains, the care of sheep and goats.
The work is hard, farmers, and the praise well-earned.
I too am at work, trusting in the power of language
To open a narrow theme and present its truth.
A happy compulsion, which makes the labour sweet,
Drives me across steep hillsides and empty uplands
Where no path runs, to find the enlivening spring.

Help me, Pales, to do justice to my theme.
The first rule with sheep is to keep them under cover
And feed them on hay till the spring grass starts to grow.
Spread the floor comfortably with straw and bracken
Shaken from its bundles; see that the flock is protected
From frosty weather, or scab and footrot will follow.
You should graze your goats where leafy arbutus grows
And where they can find their way to fresh-running water.
Let their pens face south to catch the winter sun,
Sheltered from the icy wind that February brings
When Aquarius sets and the year goes out in rain.
Goats should be no less carefully tended than sheep
And are equally useful, however high the price
That wool may fetch when dyed with Tyrian scarlet.
They bear more young, give a greater yield of milk.
The pail that foams beneath a goat's drained udder
Stands fuller when next you press the spurting teats.
But goats are good for shearing as well as milking:
The white tufted beard and the shaggy pelt
Make cloth for tents and coats for shivering sailors.
They graze the woods and ridges, content to feed
On brambles and spiky shrubs in crannies of rocks.
They keep their young close, make their own way back
To the pen, their udders scarcely clearing the floor.
All the more reason, since they give so little trouble,
That when the weather turns icy and blizzards blow
You should bring them under cover and fetch good hay
In bales from the loft to see them through the winter.
But when with low-voiced breezes the summer landscape
Calls out both flocks, the sheep and the goats, to pasture,
Set out with them early across the chilly fields.
You share the morning with the sky's most vivid star,
Dew whitens the grass, and the grazing is at its best.
After four hours, when thirst has changed the freshness
And cicadas burst the thickets with rasping song,

Water your flock where the wooden troughs are filled
With fresh supplies from a well or an undried pool.
Shelter from the midday heat in a wooded valley
Where a great oak spreads its branches against the sun
Secure in strength and age, or a grove of ilex,
Dark-leaved, rests in itself, mysteriously shaded.
Then let the flock drink again and graze till sunset,
When the air softens at the touch of the evening star.
A dewy moon rises to refresh the meadows,
The kingfisher calls by water, small birds from the wood.

Need I set my poem to tracking Libya's shepherds
Into their grazing grounds, where from scattered encampments
Day and night from one month's end to the next
The flock moves onward across the face of the desert
That stretches wide around and offers no shelter?
All that he needs the African takes with him,
His tent, gods, weapons, and at his heels his dog;
Burdened like a steady soldier fighting for Rome
Who can pitch camp after a forced march and stand ready
For battle before the enemy knows he has come.
Not so for the tribes of Scythia by Lake Maeotis,
Where the cloudy Danube twists its yellow sands
Or where Rhodope runs northward to meet the pole.
Flocks there are kept penned up in stalls. Outside
Not a blade of grass shows through. The trees stand bare.
The frozen earth founders under ten-foot drifts
And snowy dunes are blown into random shapes
By the north wind's stirring. No pause in winter there –
Through leaden mist the eyes cannot see to tell
Whether the sun lifts boldly through the morning sky
Or waters his horses at dusk in the crimson sea.
Sudden crusts fasten across the river's current.
Now water must bear the weight of chafing wheels
As heavy wagons trundle where ships once sailed.
The cold can shatter bronze; it stiffens clothes
On the wearer's back, turns pools to blocks of ice,
Freezes wine till an axe must be found to break it,
And braids men's tangled beards with icicles.
Snow falls incessantly, crowding the whole air.
Great oxen stand unmoved, trusting in their bodies'
Slow heat to save them. Deer in a herd lie buried,
Their quickness gone, their antlers' points just showing.

No need now for hunting-dogs to track them out
Nor red-feathered ropes to scare them toward the nets.
Against drifted snow-banks the helpless quarry lies
Struggling and braying, till hunters come with knives
And heave the carcasses home with excited shouts.
Their homes are caves hollowed deep underground:
There they sit out winter in front of log-piled hearths
With a fire hot enough to burn elm trunks whole;
They wear away the dark season, gaming and drinking,
With beer and scrumpy to cheer them instead of wine.
And so they live, prisoners of an Arctic sky,
Men of wild vigour, buffeted by the wind
That cannot reach their flesh through the tawny furs.

If you keep a flock for the wool, avoid rich pastures
Or ground overgrown with prickly shrubs, burrs, thistles.
Choose your sheep for their fine unspotted fleeces.
Take care with the ram. He may be of the purest white,
But if his tongue shows black under his moist palate
The lambs he fathers will be born with patched coats:
Turn him away, and search the fields for another.
With the lure of a gleaming fleece, the story has it,
Arcadian Pan once tricked you, Goddess of the moon.
You came at his call. He caught you deep in the woods.

If it is milk that you want, gather clover or trefoil
And put it in the pens by forkfuls, mixed with salt.
This raises the flock's thirst, distends their udders,
And adds subtly to the flavour of the milk.
Some goatherds wean kids early, keep them from sucking
By fastening a spiked muzzle around their mouths.
At night the milk of the morning is curded and pressed;
This they keep. But cheese from the evening milking
Is sent next day to market, fresh in its baskets,
Or seasoned with a touch of salt and laid by for winter.

You must make it your concern to keep good dogs,
Pedigree mastiffs, hounds from Sparta, bred up
On fattening whey. Such guards as these at night
Will spare you worries: a thief in the outbuildings,
The attack of mountain robbers or prowling wolves.
With your dogs you may hunt the timorous wild ass,
The hind with her springy step or the bounding hare.

Their barking starts the boar from his muddy covert
Or sends the great stag plunging across the hillside,
Bulky in his grace, and chides him into the nets.

To clear your stables of vermin burn scented cedar.
Drive stinking water-snakes off with resinous fumes.
A viper may slide beneath the uncleaned pens
And curl there, scared of daylight, dangerous to touch;
Or an adder, the kind that loves closed shady places,
That sucks at the teats of cows and scatters poison,
May hug the ground. Quick, shepherd, grab sticks and stones;
As he rears in anger, hisses and puffs his neck,
Strike at him! Already his head and half his length
Have vanished into the ground, while the tapering coils
Of the tail unwreath themselves and are drawn after.
There is also the vicious snake from Calabria's hills
Who stands erect on his body's scaly writhings,
The length of his belly mottled with dark spots.
While the rivers run in their courses above the stones
And rainy breezes freshen the earth in spring,
He keeps his greedy hunting to the banks and pools,
His black throat crammed with fish and chattering frogs.
But once the mud-cracked shallows have been baked dry,
He flickers out over the fields, his eyes discoloured,
Restless in his thirst and terrified by the heat.
I would not have him catch me asleep in the open
Or stretched in grass in a cranny of the woods,
When, his skin just shed, he leaves his young or his eggs
And slithers from the nest, bright with recovered youth,
And darts his split tongue and lifts to face the sun.

I will deal now with diseases, their causes and symptoms.
Scab attacks sheep in frosty winter weather
When freezing rain has chilled and soaked them through,
Or after shearing when the unwashed sweat still clings
And brambles rasp at their unprotected bodies.
To prevent this, the careful shepherd dips his flock,
The ram with the ewes, plunging him in the pool –
The stream carries him along, drenching his fleece.
Or he rubs the shorn bodies with an ointment prepared
From various ingredients, the bitter lees of oil,
Silver-scum, natural sulphur, pitch, oily wax,
Strong hellebore, bulbous squill or black bitumen.

Once scab gets a hold, the most effective remedy
Is to lance the sore and lay it open to the air.
The infection can only get worse by being hidden;
Festers while you hesitate to wield the knife.
No use sitting still and wishing the sickness away.
Even when the pain of it races through their bones
And has fastened on their flesh and set them bleating
With its dry fury, the fever can be reduced
By slitting a vein in the hoof-cleft and letting it bleed;
As Scythian shepherds do, or the fierce Geloni
When they wander in Rhodope or the Thracian wild
And live off sour milk mixed with horses' blood.
If a sheep stands at distance and will not leave the shade
Or grazes dully, cropping the tips of grassblades,
Or lags behind the flock and lies in the meadows
All day without moving, and is last to come in at night,
Slaughter her at once, before she spreads her sickness
And makes the harmless flock suffer for her fault.
As storm-squalls run across the surface of the sea
Disease comes thick and fast, not killing sheep singly;
It scatters their bodies up and down the pasture,
Destroys the whole flock together, ewes with their lambs.
The Alpine uplands, castled with villages,
Through Noricum, by Timavus, belonged once to shepherds.
Disease struck years ago. But the pens are empty,
The fields and hill-slopes run to waste ungrazed.

That year, autumn stood still in the plague-ridden sky
And brooded over the land with an ogreish glare.
It killed every kind of beast, the wild and the tame,
Polluted the waters, poisoned the grazing grounds.
Death was not quick nor clean; a thirst like fire
Ran through the stricken creatures and huddled their limbs;
The dryness passed; then a dropsy washed their bones
And drew the softening substance into itself.
The victim ox, standing at the altar, crowned
With the white woollen circlet of sacrifice,
Broke the slow ceremony and fell down dying.
Or if he fell to the priest's knife at his throat
The altar fire would not burn beneath the entrails
And the seer, when consulted, could give no reply.
The blood was scarcely enough to colour the knife
Or stain the sanded floor with a watery trickle.

Everywhere calves lay dying, shut in full stalls,
Or out at pasture, the rich grass all about them.
Quiet-tempered dogs ran mad. A wheezing cough
Shook pigs through their whole bulk and choked their breathing.
Even the champion racehorse lost his courage,
Refused grass and water, listlessly pawed the ground.
His ears drooped and a fitful sweat broke out there.
The sweat turned chilly – a fatal sign – and his skin
Felt dry and hard beneath the hand that stroked it.
These were symptoms that horses showed in the first days;
But as the disease gathered strength to make an end,
Their breath was fetched deep down, came heavy with groans;
Their eyes began to blaze, their flanks to heave
With long-drawn sobs; blood ran black from their nostrils;
Their tongues grew rough and stuck in their swollen throats.
Wine gave relief at first, poured through a horn;
But the hope was momentary; the draught's effect
Was to bring them nearer death, stoking their fever
And filling them with false strength – God give such strength
To makers of mischief, keep it from all good men –
And they bit and tore at themselves with naked teeth.
Steaming under the weight of the plough, the bullock
Collapsed; blood mixed with foam slid from his mouth;
He groaned life out. What else could the ploughman do
But unyoke the grieving partner and lead him away,
Leaving the furrow unfinished, the share in the soil?
The steep shadows of hillsides, the open meadows,
The pouring of streams from rocks to the low fields,
Could not stir the animals. Their skin lay loose
On their hollow flanks, a dull look thickened their eyes;
They had no strength left even to lift their heads.
What help was it to have spent their lives at the plough?
Though men may spoil their bodies with food and drink,
Stretched out like bloated carcasses at the feast,
The diet of these was leaves, the grass at their feet;
They drank fresh water from the quick-flowing rivers
And springs; they slept the sleep of unthinking health.
At this time only there were no cows to be found
For the rites of Juno; an ill-matched shambling pair
Of buffalo drew her car with gifts to the shrine.
Men picked the earth over painfully with mattocks;
They dug in the seed with their nails; with straining necks
They hauled the creaking wagons over the hillpaths.

No wolves hung about the folds or prowled at night
Looking for sheep to take. They had been subdued
By a nearer worry. Timorous hinds, shy stags
Wandered among the house-dogs and came to the door.
Waves strewed the beaches with the remains of creatures
Washed up dead from the sea like shipwrecked corpses.
Seals swam up along the rivers, strangers after safety.
The startled water-snake bristled his scales; the viper
Lay sick to death, unsheltered in his winding hole.
Birds found the sky no sanctuary; a gust of wind
Blew their light lives away – they died on the wing.
No change of pasture brought relief, no cure
Given by Melampus, Amythaon's son, nor Chiron,
Son of Phillyra; the remedy fed the plague.
It was as if a Fury of Vengeance had broken loose
Bringing disease and terror from their shadowy place
To parade with her in daylight, greedily vaunting.
The hill-slopes and dried river-hollows echoed
The bleating of sheep, the ceaseless lowing of cattle.
So many died that the stables were piled with corpses
Which melted in rotting heaps. Nothing could be saved.
It was best, men found, to bury them deep in pits.
No washing in fresh water, no searing in fire
Would cleanse or purge the flesh; the hide was useless.
They could scarcely shear the fleece, decayed as it was
With sores and filth. Woven, the cloth fell apart.
If anyone brought himself to wear such a garment,
Burning ulcers would break out across his body;
A rank sweat bathed him; and he had not long to wait
Before the plague was shooting flames through his joints.

Georgic 4

Let me sweeten my poem with honey for its theme,
The gift of the sky. Permit me now, Maecenas,
To present for your entertainment a miniature state:
I will give an account of its fierce-hearted leaders,
Its orderly tribes, their manners, their pursuits, their wars.
Is the subject too slight? Who will slight a poet's pains
If gods do not grudge him and Apollo hears his call?

First you must settle on a place to put the hives –
Look for a sheltered spot, not used for grazing.
Wind prevents bees from carrying home their food;
Sheep and goats beat the flowers down; wandering cattle
Scatter field-dew and wear the rich turf thin.
Keep away the lizards with bright green scaly backs
And harmful birds, the bee-eater and the swallow,
Its breast-feathers stained by Procne's hands for a sign.
These do great damage, snatching bees from flight –
Sweet morsels to stop their nestlings' gaping throats.
There should be water close by, pools green with moss
And a small stream running shallowly through the grass.
Let a palm or large wild olive shade the entrance –
When new kings lead out the swarms in early spring
To claim their season, and young bees play about the hives
The slope nearby will offer shelter from the heat
And the spread branches extend a leafy welcome.
You should bridge the water, whether a stream or pool,
With stones or leaning willows, so that the bees
Have a surface where they can settle, opening their wings
To the sun when a showery gust has slowed their flight
Or a sudden cloudburst drenched and beaten them down.
Plant herbs around, green casia, powerful thyme
And savory with its breath that steeps the air.
Let banks of violets dabble their leaves by the stream.
To construct the hives, use insulating cork
Or a close framework of interwoven twigs.
Make the entrances narrow, otherwise the honey
Will solidify in cold weather and melt in summer.
Bees suffer from both extremes. It is not for nothing
That they labour to stop the tiny chinks in their walls,
To seal the crevices, binding the wax with a gum

Gathered from flowers and kept for this special use –
A glue more tenacious than birdlime or Phrygian pitch.
It is said that bees will tunnel their homes for warmth
In underground recesses, and they have been found
In pumice rock and cavities of hollow trees.
Help them by smearing gaps in their chambers with clay
And scattering leaves on the top to keep them warm.
There must be no yews growing near the hive, no fire
Where reddened crab-shells are burnt, no marshy ground,
No patch of foul-smelling mud, nor hollow cliffside
Where a shout jumps back, like steel, as it strikes the rocks.

When the gold sun has driven winter underground
And filled the summer sky with resistless light
Bees scatter among the glades and wooded slopes –
They harvest the newly opened flowers, they hover
And sip at the streams; then, delighting in their instinct,
Return to foster their young in the hive, to fashion
Cells of fresh wax and form the clammy honey.
When you look up and see a swarm on its first journey
Floating skyward through the clear summer air,
An indistinctness, a dark spot that trails in the breeze,
Watch it as it goes. Fresh water, leafy shade –
Their search is always the same. Take care then to bait them
With the scents prescribed, crushed balm and lowly honeywort.
Raise a sound of tinkling, clash Cybele's cymbals.
You will find that they settle where the herbs are spread
And occupy the hive as if they had found it themselves.

When a quarrel breaks out between two rival kings
And the bees come out to battle, swarm against swarm,
Their minds restless, their hearts trembling for the fight,
You can hear from a field away the raucous buzzing
Which upbraids stragglers, and a strident broken note
As if bronze trumpets were blowing calls to arms.
Hastily the forces muster. They flash their wings,
Sharpen their stings and limber up to attack,
Gathering thick about their monarch's tent-royal
And taunting the enemy with loud battle-cries.
So on a clear spring day they burst from their gates
To skirmish across the open fields of air.
They clash, and the battle-fury echoes high overhead,
Then cluster into one great ball and tumble earthward

As thick as hailstones or acorns shaken from an oak.
Where the fighting is thickest, the kingly champions spread
Their glittering wings, great souls in little bodies,
Determined, both of them, to fight to the end –
Till their last soldier has left them, or the field is won.
Yet their high passions, their desperate encounters
Are easily quietened by flinging a handful of dust.

Once you have stopped the fighting and recalled both captains,
Destroy the weaker one – weakness brings waste –
And leave the stronger to reign unchallenged in the hive.
You will know him by the burning spots of yellow gold.
Bees come in two kinds: one is better, of finer make,
With scales that catch the light; the other has a dull look,
Is sloth's victim, and drags his paunch as he goes.
In this division the commoners are like the kings,
Some shabby and dishevelled, like a man without water
Caught by a wind-flurry on a dust-heaped road,
Spitting dirt from his dry mouth. Others flash and glisten –
Their sleek bodies are patterned with flecks of gold,
Their children stronger, their honey sweet and liquid
– It will take the edge off the sharpness of new wine.
Season by season you will press it from the combs.

But when the bees fly aimlessly, playing in the air,
Forgetting the combs and letting the hives grow cold,
You must stop this indulgence, break their idle mood.
It is simply done. Take the king and pull off his wings.
When the general is crippled, the soldiers will not venture –
Goodbye to the fighting field and the perilous voyage.
Let them stay where the garden breathes its yellow bloom;
Where Priapus stands, old Hellespontine watchman,
With a willow sickle to scare off birds and thieves.
To make a proper job of it, a bee-keeper
Must be a gardener too. He must collect wild thyme,
Pine seedlings from the hills, and flowering shrubs,
Plant them with his own hands and keep them watered.

If there were still time (my poem draws to its close,
I take in sail, shift course, and make for the shore)
I might speak of the tended beauty of orchard-gardens,
Of Paestum rosebeds that flower twice in a year,
How the endive relishes the stream it drinks,

How parsley lines the banks, how the marrow swells
Its belly in tangled grass. I would find a place too
For the late-flowering daffodil, the twined acanthus,
For seaward myrtle and ivy with white-streaked leaves.
I remember seeing beneath the high towers of Tarentum
Where Galaesus flows black through yellowing fields of corn
An old man from Corycus. He had a small patch of ground
And little besides – no ploughing there for oxen,
No space for sheep, and the soil unfriendly to vines.
Thorntrees possessed the ground, until he planted
White lilies, herbs, vervain and slender poppies –
A little kingdom. He would come in past nightfall
And load his table with food – not a scrap of it bought.
He was first with roses in spring, with apples in autumn.
Before winter's end, while sharp frosts cracked the rocks
And streams ran chained by ice, he had coaxed the hyacinth
To flower, and shorn it of the delicate bloom,
And was scolding the late year, the unsoftening winds.
He was earliest among his neighbours to stock the hives
With new-hatched bees, and to draw off foaming honey
From the pressed combs. He had groves of lime and pine.
His orchard trees brought all their fruit to ripeness,
As many as they promised in the blossoming spring.
He would plant trees out in rows though they were far-grown:
The elm, the prickly sloe, the hardening pear,
The planetree that roofed drinkers with its airy shade.
Let this memory stand for all I might say of gardens;
The saying must wait for others, while I hasten on.

Let me speak now of that special instinct, not inborn
But given to bees by Jupiter as a reward
When they followed the Curetes' percussive music
And fed the King of Heaven in the Dictaean Cave.
Bees are the only creatures to share their young,
To live in a common home by established laws,
And to have their own country, their ancestral gods.
Never forgetting winter, they labour through the year
To lay up what they can for the use of all.
They divide their duties. Some work across the fields
Searching for food. Others, shut in the hive,
Compound the dews of self-regarding narcissus
With bark-bled resin to build foundations of combs
And hang the clinging wax. Some lead out the young,

Their tribe's best hope. Others pack the pure honey
Filling the new-made cells with unearthly sweetness.
There are those whose job it is to guard the gates,
To watch the weather, the approach of clouds and showers,
To unload those coming in, or else to join ranks
And drive the drones, a lazy herd, from the hive.
What heat of labour! How the honey smells of thyme!
Imagine how the Cyclopses fashion stubborn ore
Into thunderbolts – some work the bull-hide bellows,
Others plunge the hissing metal in cold water;
All Etna rumbles to the shock of hammer on anvil
As the hurrying team lift their gigantic arms
In violent rhythm, and the iron is turned in the tongs.
Set the demigod and the insect side by side –
They are both of them driven creatures. Passion for gain
Compels each bee to its task. The old are employed
As master craftsmen to construct the maze of combs.
The younger come back weary in the last of dusk,
Their thighs yellow with pollen. All day they have browsed
On arbutus, thyme, grey willow, oozing linden,
Lavender, fiery saffron and leaf-marked orchid.
All share their time of labour, their time of rest.
At dawn they rush from the gates – no hesitance then.
When evening gives the sign, they leave the fields
As promptly, and come back to refresh their bodies,
Humming around the hive as they wait to enter.
They settle in their chambers. The murmur fades.
Night deepens, and their tired limbs belong to sleep.
When rain hangs in the sky or the wind sharpens
From the east, the bees are cautious, keep close to home.
They draw water in the shelter of their city walls,
Make brief forays, and take up tiny stones.
With these they steady their flight through buffeting air
Like small boats taking ballast when the sea is rough.
But of all the customs of bees the strangest is this:
That the pleasure of sex, its annihilating sweetness,
And the pain of giving birth mean nothing to them.
They find their young among leaves and scented herbs,
Gathering a new king and little citizens
To restore the palaces of their waxen kingdom.
As they wander they may tear their wings on sharp-edged rocks
But will not let go their burden. It is stronger than life –
The honey-passion that drives them from flower to flower.

Though their time on earth is short and crowded with risk
– None of them survives more than seven years –
The race they spring from persists and gathers glory,
And they die, as their forbears died, that it should live.
What is more, their devotion to their kings surpasses
The prostrate reverence of Egypt and the east.
So long as the king is safe, he unites them all.
But once he is lost, they dissolve their society,
Break their handiwork, pull down the trellised combs.
He is master of their labours and has their homage.
They crowd around him, carry him shoulder-high
Amid fierce acclamation; lightly they turn
To seek in battle for wounds and a loyal death.

Observing these patterns, their intricacy, their justness,
Some men conclude that bees, as they drink the air,
Draw in with it a trace of divine intention.
They say that a spirit fills earth and sky and sea;
That man and his fellow-creatures, the wild and the tame,
Take from it the delicate stuff of their life.
There is no dying, they believe, when the body fails;
But, released, the life leaps lightly away to its place
In the depth of heaven, a brightness pointing the stars.

Before you lift the honey from its treasure chamber
Wash yourself well and gargle to sweeten your breath.
Bring smoke to drive the bees from their narrow home.
There are two seasons for taking the gathered harvest –
The first when Taygete, the clear-faced Pleiad star,
Rises from Ocean – he cannot hold her back –
And later, when she flies gloomily from the sign
Of the watery Fish, to set in the winter sea.
The rage of bees is ungovernable. When hurt
They will leave their barbed stings hidden in the flesh,
Parting with their lives in the wounds that they inflict.

If you worry that a hard winter may break their strength
And you pity their danger, be sparing in what you take,
But fumigate the combs with thyme and cut them back
When empty – otherwise parasite drones will move in
And cockroaches swarm there to escape the light of day.
The newt will feed unnoticed on the waxen cells,
The hornet look for the fight he is sure to win.

Moth will make havoc, and the spider loathed by Pallas
Will curtain the disused doorways with loose-hung webs.
The more their supplies are drained, the more eagerly
Bees work, the whole tribe together, to fend off ruin,
Still bringing pollen to restore the galleried combs.

But, for all their courage, bees know the worst of life,
Just as men do. Disease may sap their strength.
You can tell its approach by unmistakeable symptoms.
Those that are sick immediately change colour
And a lean ragged look deforms their countenance.
They carry the dead from the hive in sad procession,
Or else hang at the entrance with clinging feet
Or loiter in the hive together, unable to move,
Faint from hunger and stunned by pinching cold.
They make a duller sound, a long-drawn buzzing
Like the south wind when it stirs coldly among woods
Or the chafed sea hissing with the undertow of waves
Or fire as it heaves and roars in a closed furnace.
My advice would be to set a sweet gum smouldering
And to give them boiled honey in hollows of reeds,
Inviting them to forget their sickness and eat.
It may help to add the flavour of pounded oak-galls
And dried rose-petals, or wine thickened over a fire,
Or a syrup made of raisins from the Psithian vine,
Or Athenian thyme and sharp-smelling centaury.
There is also a plant growing wild in the meadows
Which country people call starwort. It is easy to find.
From its matted roots it sends up a forest of stalks.
The disk of the flower is gold. The surrounding petals
Have a purple glint beneath their violet blackness.
Woven into wreaths, it adorns the altars of the gods.
It has the rough taste of my boyhood: shepherds would gather it
In the smooth-grazed valleys and on Mella's winding banks.
Boil up the roots of this plant with sweet-smelling wine
And place them in baskets by the doorways of the hive.

But in case the stock should be wiped out all at once
And you see no way by which to repair the loss,
You should know about the Arcadian master's adventure,
How he discovered that the corrupted blood
Of slaughtered oxen will produce a swarm of bees:
I will trace the story to its legendary source.

From where the people of Canopus and Pella mingle
By the generous waters of the flooded Nile
And farmers make their rounds in painted skiffs,
To where the great river emerges from Africa,
Setting a boundary against the Persian bowmen
And fertilizing the green land with black loam
Before it pours itself out through seven mouths –
The whole of Egypt puts its trust in this art.
They choose a confined space suited to their purpose
And enclose it with four walls and a narrow roof.
In each of the walls they make a slanted window
Just wide enough to let in light and air.
Then they take a two-year-old bullock with curving horns,
Block up both his nostrils, gag his mouth –
He will struggle but they do it – and beat him to death.
The skin must remain whole though the flesh is crushed.
They put the carcase in the cell with branches around
And beneath it, and scatter rosemary and thyme.
This is done as the west wind begins to ruffle the waters,
Before the meadows get back their colour and growth
Or twittering martins hang their nests from the eaves.
As the liquid warms and ferments in the bruised bones,
Creatures miraculously stir from the carrion.
At first they are limbless; soon they cluster in a swarm
On buzzing wings and try short flights through the air;
Then they break away suddenly, like a summer cloudburst
Or a shower of arrows loosed from twanging bowstrings
When light-armed Parthians stand their ground and fight.

What god showed us this discovery, gracious Muses?
Where does it come from, our appetite for invention?
The story tells how the shepherd Aristaeus left Tempe
Where hunger and sickness had destroyed his bees,
And tracking the River Peneus, came to its source.
There, full of trouble, he stood by the spring and spoke:
'Mother, Cyrene, embodiment of clear water,
Is this what it means to be the son of a god?
Could Apollo rest in Thymbra and let me be ruined?
Is he truly my father? And what has become of your love?
How can I hope for my promised place in the sky
When the proudest achievement of my life on earth,
Those arts of husbandry which my care and resource
Have scarcely mastered, must be set aside, abandoned...

Tear up my plantations of trees with your own hands,
Set hostile fire to my barns, destroy my harvests,
Burn my seedlings and take an axe to my vines.
How deep my offence if these should win me praise!'
His outcry came to her as she sat in her chamber
On the riverbed, her Nymphs at work around her
Carding rich fleeces as smooth and green as glass:
Drymo and Xantho, Ligaea and Phyllodoce,
Their gleaming hair tumbled loose on their white necks;
Cydippe and blonde Lycorias, the one still virgin,
The other newly racked by Lucina's pangs;
Clio and her sister Beroe, daughters of Ocean,
With their dappled animal skins, their golden ornaments;
Ephyre and Opis, Deiopea from the Asian meadow,
And quick Arethusa, her arrows at last laid aside.
Among them Clymene, who sang the ballad of Mars
And Vulcan, the deluded ambush and sweet disgrace.
From Chaos on, she untangled the loves of gods,
And lost in her song they drew out the delicate thread
On their spindles. But again the cries of Aristaeus
Struck his mother's ears; the company of Nymphs sat stunned
On their glassy seats. Arethusa, the soonest to stir,
Swam up, broke surface with her blonde hair, looked out
And called back across the distance, 'Cyrene, sister,
You had good cause to be frightened. It is your son,
Aristaeus, your darling, who stands on the riverbank
And shouts your name and accuses you through his tears.'
His mother felt a fresh shock of worry and answered,
'Bring him down to us, bring him down, it is allowed
That he cross into our mystery,' and she told the waters
To draw aside to give the young shepherd passage.
Like the walls of a mountain the river parted round him,
Took him to its depths, and closed in a hollow above.
He found himself, a stranger, in his mother's house,
A place of caves, lakes, echoes, pillared groves,
Dazed by the bulk of waters, deafened by the noise;
And saw the rivers of the earth as they came rushing
Along their hidden courses; saw Phasis and Lycus
And the spring from which strong Enipeus bursts away;
Saw Father Tiber and Anio green with sulphur,
Mysian Caicus, Hypanis loud among rocks,
And Eridanus, bull-headed, with golden horns,
Cutting through rich lowlands to spend his strength

In the turmoiled sea, the most powerful river of all.
Once he had reached the chamber with stone-hung roof
And Cyrene had learnt the cause of his empty tears,
The sisters waited on him. Some brought pure water
To rinse his hands, some fetched soft towels to dry them,
Some loaded tables with food and filled the cups.
The altars flowered with incense, Panchaean flames,
And his mother said, 'Take a cup of wine in your hands
And spill a libation to Ocean.' With that she prayed
To Ocean, earliest of gods, and the Nymphs, her sisters,
Who guard a hundred forests and a hundred streams.
Three times over she dowsed the hearth-fire with wine.
Each time the low flames flared to the roof of the cave.
She cheered him with this omen; then she began,
'There is an old man called Proteus, a sea-green wizard
Who lives in the waters of Carpathus. He rides a chariot
Drawn by a team of two-legged fish-tailed horses.
He has gone to the coast of Emathia now, to visit
His homeground, Pallene. Old Nereus and us Nymphs
Reverence his gift. He knows all there is to be known.
Past, present and future lie open to him, equally clear.
So Neptune settled it, and gave him a lumbering flock
Of gross sleek seals to shepherd on the bed of the sea.
Take him prisoner, child. Force him to say why your bees
Fell sick, and how you may turn your trouble to good.
He will give no help unless forced. Entreaty to him
Means nothing. But chain him, break him, and he is yours;
With all his tricks he must yield at last to constraint.
In the heat of midday, when grass wilts and the flocks
Gather in the narrowing shade and forget to graze,
He comes from the sea, stretches out in a hidden cove
And sleeps – I will show you the place. You must take him then.
Once mastered by your grip and bound in fetters
He will baffle you with animal and elemental shapes,
Change in a moment to a tigress, a bristled boar,
A tawny-pelted lioness, a smooth-scaled snake;
Turn to sharp fire that hisses about your ears,
Turn to thin water slipping through the links of his chains.
But however he varies himself amid crowding forms
Pull the fetters tighter, child, and hold him down
Till with a last change his body recovers its shape,
As it was at first when he lay unguarded and slept.'
As she spoke, she shed a heavenly scent about her

Which bathed her son's body from head to foot
And breathed from his braided hair. He stood transfigured.
Strength filled his limbs.
                                        There is an enormous cavern
Hollowed from a cliff-side where, wave on wind-driven wave,
The sea divides and breaks among deep-set coves –
A place where sailors shelter to ride out storms.
There, among vast boulders, Proteus has his den.
The Nymph hid the youth in a cranny away from the light
And then withdrew and wrapped herself in cloud.
It was a midsummer noon. The parching sun
Stood like a fiery keystone at the top of his arch.
The rapid Dog-Star blazed. The meadows lay brown.
Mud steamed and dried in the stagnant river-hollows.
Returning to the cavern as usual, Proteus emerged
From water, surrounded by his clumsy flock
Scattering spray as they frisked and rolled about him.
They lay down to sleep here and there along the shore,
While like an upland herdsman watching his fold
At dusk when cattle are brought in from pasture
And wolves prick up their ears at the wailing of lambs,
He sat above on a rock and counted them over.
Aristaeus waited, impatient for his chance.
The old man had scarcely stretched out his tired limbs
When he let out a great shout and burst from ambush
And had him in fetters. Then passionate to evade,
The wizard tried all his magic, tried every shape,
Fire, beast, water, in a continual change;
But when he found no way out and knew himself beaten
He ceased struggling, took back his own shape, and spoke:
'What do you want from me, insolent young man?
Who set you on to attack me in my lair?'
'Let there be no more pretending,' Aristaeus answered.
'You know who brought me here. You know why I came.
Give me an oracle, Proteus, to explain my loss.'
At this the trapped seer's eyes rolled and blazed
With emerald light. Angrily he ground his teeth.
Then the story that had to be told broke from his lips.

'An avenging spirit pursues you, crazed by grief,
The ghost of Orpheus, calling for his lost bride.
If the punishment that he gives you matched your crime
The troubles you suffer now would seem like joys.

Remember how the doomed girl fled, how you ran her down
In the deep grass by the river, and she could not see
The enormous viper that lay along the bank at her feet.
The Dryad girls, missing her from their mountain dances,
Began to wail. From Rhodope to Pangaea,
On northern heights, by Hebrus, through warring Thrace,
Where Orithyia wanders in exile, the cry went up.
On the empty seashore Orpheus tuned his anguish
To the hollow lyre, shaping his song to the pattern
Of her beauty, the absence that haunted him day and night.
He entered Taenarus, the cavernous gate of Dis,
And found his way through the black and fearful maze
To face the King of the Dead in his ghostly kingdom
Where all prayers fail and hearts are dead as stones.
He gathered an audience of shadows to hear him sing
And made them feel again. From the crannies of Erebus
They flocked about him like birds that hide in the leaves
When dusk or breaking weather drives them from the hills –
Grown men and women, strengthless forms of heroes
Drained of their brimming life, young boys and girls,
Young men set on the pyre while their parents watched –
Imprisoned beyond black mud and jagged reeds
And stagnant water, the clogged stream of Cocytus,
Wound in hateful coils by the ninefold Styx.
His music thrilled through the lowest pit of Tartarus
Quieting the Furies, their blue hair writhed with snakes,
The snapping jaws of the three-headed Dog hung loose…
The wind dropped and Ixion's wheel stood still.
And now, all dangers passed, he had brought her back.
She followed behind him obedient to Proserpine
And felt the breeze of the world already in her face
When a passion for reassurance gripped his heart
(A weakness to be forgiven, if ghosts could forgive).
On the verge of day he stopped. Light dazed his will.
Was she his again? He turned, he looked, he broke
The harsh condition; in that moment his labour was lost.
Three dry crashes of thunder rolled across Avernus
And she spoke to him, "Your thoughtlessness in love,
Orpheus, has wrecked us both. The current of fate
Catches me, it pulls me backward, my blurred eyes swim.
Goodbye, goodbye! I am lost in a huge darkness.
My hands have no strength, no substance, to catch at yours."
These were her last words. Smoke that thins and scatters

In the breeze, she was fading, vanishing before his eyes,
Was gone. He started after her, catching at shadows,
With everything still to say. But the ferryman of Orcus
Stood in his path, and would not give him passage.
What skill had he to master this second loss?
What tears, what song might win him the gods' reprieve?
Styx lay impassably between her and her life.
Month after month, for seven whole months, men say,
He meditated his grief among cliffs and caves
Along Strymon's icy course, with no one by.
Tigers fawned on him, oaktrees followed to hear him.
He sang as a nightingale sings in the poplar shade
Keening for her lost brood of unfeathered young
Which a rough ploughman has found and pulled from the nest.
Perched on a branch, she returns on her song through the night
Filling the landscape with long-drawn painful notes.
No love, no marriage-rite could waylay his mind.
Over mountains, rivers, plains, he wandered northward
Lost in a world never widowed of its snows
– Eurydice's absence and the empty gift of Dis –
Till one night of orgy the women of the Cicones,
Furious that he stood apart from their holy lust,
Tore his young body and scattered it through the fields.
His wrenched-off head they flung in the River Hebrus,
Whose current rolled it through the land where he was born.
"Eurydice", he shouted – nothing remained but a voice –
"Eurydice", her name still alive on his cold tongue,
While from bank to bank the broad stream echoed his cry.'
Here Proteus finished, threw himself clear, dived down.
The sea closed above him in a whirling rush of foam.

But Cyrene stayed. She spoke to her terrified son,
'Your trouble is over, child. You have your answer.
The disease has a simple cause, a simple cure.
The Nymphs Eurydice danced with in upland woods
Have sent this plague on your bees. You must offer gifts
And make your peace with them. They are quick to forgive
And with prayer and worship soon put by their anger.
But first you must learn the proper rites of entreaty.
Pick out four of your handsomest bulls, the largest
That you have at pasture on the Arcadian hills,
Take as many heifers, untouched by the yoke,
And raise four altars by the shrine of the Nymphs.

Cut their throats, let the sacred blood run down,
And leave their carcasses in a woodland clearing.
Let eight days pass. On the morning of the ninth
Give the ghost of Orpheus poppies to make him forget,
Sacrifice a black lamb, and go back to the clearing...
Then offer a calf to Eurydice's reconciled shade.'
No lingering as he followed his mother's commands:
He came to the shrine, raised altars as she told him,
Led four of his handsomest bulls to the sacrifice,
And as many heifers, untouched by the yoke.
The eight days passed. On the morning of the ninth
He offered Orpheus his dues and went back to the clearing.
And there an astonishing portent met men's eyes.
In the rotten bowels of the cattle, in their swollen bellies
And bursting from their sides, bees buzzed and swarmed.
In a cloud they trailed skyward, settled on a treetop,
Hung from the bending branches like a cluster of grapes.

Here is my poem about fields and flocks and trees.
I made it while great Caesar thundered in war
By the deep Euphrates; while he conquered, judged, gave laws
To willing nations, and drove beyond earthly glory.
All this time, in Parthenope's kind city,
I, Virgil, laboured to strengthen my youthful art,
Who once made play with shepherds' improvised verses
And sang you, Tityrus, stretched in the beechtree's shade.

8
Theocritus
The Idylls

1   *The Passion of Daphnis*

THYRSIS

That pinetree by the spring and your touch on the pipe:
Both whisper a music to draw the listener in
With its sweetness, goatherd. Only Pan plays sweeter.
If he chooses the horned goat, you shall take the she-goat
For your prize. If he takes the she-goat, the kid shall be yours.
It tastes delicious, the flesh of an unmilked kid.

GOATHERD

Your song is sweeter, shepherd, than the waternoise
Made by the stream tumbling from its rocky spout.
If the Muses claim the ewe as a gift, you shall have
The plump pet lamb. If they want the plump pet lamb
You shall take the sheep, and be second only to them.

THYRSIS

Sit down now, goatherd, (think the Nymphs had asked you)
And play your pipe, here where the hillside steepens
And tamarisks grow on the slope. I will watch your goats.

GOATHERD

There must be no piping at midday, shepherd, none:
We are scared of Pan. Now is the time when he rests
Tired out from the morning's hunting. He can turn nasty,
Tilting his nose at us, quick to take offence.
But, Thyrsis, you have composed 'The Passion of Daphnis'
And have made yourself a master of herdsmen's song.
Let's sit underneath this elm, with the glade before us:
There Priapus stands, there water spreads and gushes
By the oaks and the shepherds' bench set into the hill.
If you sing as you did in the match with Libyan Chromis
I will let you have a goat that can suckle twins
And fill two pails besides, to be milked three times;
And will give you a deep, two-handled cup, new-made,
Washed in fresh wax, still fragrant from the knife.
About the lip of the cup an ivy pattern
Is carved, with golden points among the leaves:
A fluent tendril flaunting its yellow bloom.
Beneath is a woman's figure, delicately worked:
She is robed and wears a circlet to keep her hair.

On either side of her stand two bearded suitors
Arguing their claim. But she takes no notice,
Looks smilingly at one man, or so it appears,
Then at the other; while, hollow-eyed with love,
They struggle against her kindly indifference.
Beside these is carved an aged fisherman
On a jutting rock. He strains at the very edge
Of his strength to draw in a net with its heavy catch.
You can see the effort bunching in each tense limb
And in his neck as he gives himself to the task.
He has white hair, but his strength is supple and fresh.
A little distance from the old man's sea-labour
There is a vineyard hung with darkening clusters.
A small boy perches on a dry stone wall to guard them.
Two foxes shadow him. One sneaks along the rows
For plunder; another has fixed her tricky eye
On the quarter-loaf the boy keeps for his breakfast
And will not let him alone till she has snatched it.
Blithely intent, he shapes a cage for a cricket
From asphodel stalks and rushes. The bag with his food
Is forgotten; so are the vines. The toy absorbs him.
The base of the cup is overspread with acanthus.
A goatherd's treasure! It is too fine a thing.
I paid the Calydna ferryman a good price for it,
A goat, a large cheese made of the best milk.
It felt too precious to drink from; I put it away
Unused. But how cheerfully I would part with it
For that beautiful elegy. Do you think I mock you?
No holding back! You cannot take your song with you
In the end. Hades and forgetfulness are the same.

★

THYRSIS
Muses, sing for a herdsman, sing me your song.

Thyrsis from Etna asks you. Listen to his voice.

Where were you, Nymphs, when Daphnis came to grief?
What distant valley or mountain gave you delight?
You could not be found beside Anapus, the great river,
Nor by the water of Acis, nor on Etna's height.

Muses, sing for a herdsman, sing me your song.

Jackals and wolves howled their lament for Daphnis.
The lion wept in its forest-bound retreat.
Many the cattle that watched about him dying,
The bulls and cows and calves couched at his feet.

Muses, sing for a herdsman, sing me your song.

Hermes came from the mountain, said to him, 'Daphnis,
Tell me what passion hurts you. Who is to blame?'
The cowherds, shepherds and goatherds gathered round him,
'Tell us your trouble,' they asked. Old Priapus came.

Muses, sing for a herdsman, sing me your song.

'Daphnis,' he said, 'an unhappy girl goes searching
Each glade and spring for the one on whom she dotes.
Are you her lover, incompetent, feeble-hearted?
You should change your cattle and take a flock of goats;
You are no better than a goatherd, watching and pining
While the billy does his work and the nanny bleats.

Muses, sing for a herdsman, sing me your song.

'In tears you watch the girls, you hear their laughter;
Poor hobbledehoy, you long to join their dance.'
But the cowherd drew near the limit of his passion,
Deaf to taunts, absorbed in a bitter trance.

Muses, sing for a herdsman, repeat your song.

Next came Cypris, her smile sweet and empty;
Her heart was heavy, her cheerfulness a pretence.
'You boasted you were a match for Love in wrestling;
You lie there overthrown for your offence.'

Muses, sing for a herdsman, repeat your song.

Daphnis answered her, 'Tormenting Cypris,
Hateful to all men, goddess of jealous pride,
Do you think my last sun is sinking? Even in Hades
Daphnis will be the thorn in Love's sleek side.

Muses, sing for a herdsman, repeat your song.

'They say that a certain cowherd… Hurry to Ida,
Anchises lies there on a bed of galingale;
The oaks will screen you, the humming bees tell no tale.

Muses, sing for a herdsman, repeat your song.

'Adonis the shepherd-boy needs to take a lover.
He hunts the hare and chases all kinds of prey.
Go set yourself before Diomede, and tell him
"Daphnis paid for his boldness. You too must pay."

Muses, sing for a herdsman, repeat your song.

'Goodbye, you wolves and jackals, you skulking bears.
The forest-glades and thickets where you hide
Shall never see me again. Goodbye, Arethusa,
Goodbye, you streams that pour down Etna's side.
Here Daphnis fed his cattle, here he watered them:
Remember him in the place where he lived and died.

Muses, sing for a herdsman, repeat your song.

'O Pan, are you ranging the long hills of Lycaeus
Or the heights of Maenalus? Leave your ground and come
To Sicily. Leave Helice's peak and the mountain,
Cherished by the gods, where Arcas has his tomb.

Goodbye to the herdsman, Muses, goodbye to the song.

'Come, master, and take this pipe of mine, sweet-smelling,
Fastened with wax, the lip-piece delicately bound.
Love drags me into the darkness where no songs sound.

Goodbye to the herdsman, Muses, goodbye to the song.

'Bear violets now, you bramble-bushes and thorntrees,
Let the world turn cross-natured, since Daphnis dies.
Let the prickly juniper bloom with soft narcissus,
The pine be weighed with pears. Let the stag hunt the hounds,
Let the nightingale attend to the screech-owl's cries.'

Goodbye to the herdsman, Muses, goodbye to the song.

He said nothing more. Aphrodite struggled to raise him,
But the thread allowed by the Fates had run to its end.
Daphnis drew near the water and the current took him,
Unhappy child of the Muses, the Nymphs' lost friend.

Goodbye to the herdsman, Muses, goodbye to the song.

★

Now give me the goat and the carved cup. Let me milk her
And drink to the Muses.
                    Muses, goodbye, but only
For the moment! In time I shall sing you a sweeter song.

GOATHERD
Then, Thyrsis, you must stop your mouth with sweetness,
Eat only honeycomb and the best dried figs,
Since, even as it is, you out-sing the cicada.
Here is the cup. Smell the scented wood, so fresh
You would think it had been dipped at the well of the Hours.
Cissaetha!
        Yours for milking!
                        Gently, my goats,
Down! or you'll have the billy force you down.

2 Pharmaceutria

Give me the bay-leaves, Thestylis, give me the charms;
Put a circlet of fine red wool around the cup.
Hurry! I must work a spell to bind my lover.
O how he hurts me! Twelve days without a visit,
Without so much as a knock at my door to learn
If I were alive or dead. Does he care so little
Whose bed he shares? Is his love so slight? Tomorrow
I'll go down to the wrestling-school of Timagetus,
Find him and let him know how he's treated me.
But now I'll bind him with magic. Moon, shine clearly;
Listen to my song; I'll chant it low for you
And for blood-bathed Hecate, your earthly double,
From whom dogs cower as she wanders among graves.
Be with me, Hecate, queen of terrors; help me
To make these drugs as strong as any brewed
By Circe, Medea or yellow-haired Perimede.

★

Turn, magic wheel, and force my lover home.

First barley-grains must be scattered in the fire,
　　Thestylis. Do it, and as you throw them on –
Are you laughing at me, girl, or have you forgotten? –
　　Repeat, I scatter Delphis bone by bone.

Turn, magic wheel, and force my lover home.

Next I light the bay-leaves. They crackle and flare;
　　When the flame has died no trace of ash remains.
Delphis wounds me. Then let the fire seize Delphis,
　　Shrivel his heart and burn along his veins.

Turn, magic wheel, and force my lover home.

Now I throw on the corn-husks. Nothing holds fast
　　Against you, Artemis, either on earth or in hell.
The town-dogs howl; the goddess is at the crossroads.
　　Keep us safe from her, Thestylis. Strike the bell!

Turn, magic wheel, and force my lover home.

Listen, the night is windless, the sea lies still;
    Only my turmoil interrupts the calm,
My love-gone-bad for a man in love with himself,
    The thief of my happiness and my good name.

Turn, magic wheel, and force my lover home.

As this wax image melts at the goddess's prompting
    Let Myndian Delphis melt in love once more.
As the bronze blade whirrs with Aphrodite's power
    Let him hover and twist in pain about my door.

Turn, magic wheel, and force my lover home.

I make three libations and say this three times, Lady:
    May the woman or the man who shares his bed
Miss him sooner than Theseus was missed on Naxos
    When heavy-haired Ariadne woke betrayed.

Turn, magic wheel, and force my lover home.

Mares and their foals, if they eat Arcadian coltsfoot,
    Gallop in frenzy over the upland meadows.
O to see Delphis break madly from the wrestling-school
    And never stop till he burst into my house.

Turn, magic wheel, and force my lover home.

I shred the fringe that Delphis lost from his cloak
    And throw it in the brazier. Devil or god,
You stick to me, Love, like a fat leech from the marshes,
    Suck my body and drain out all the blood.

Turn, magic wheel, and force my lover home.

I'll give him juice from a lizard to drink tomorrow.
    Now, Thestylis, before the dawn comes on,
Take these ashes, crush them over his doorstep
    And whisper, I crush Delphis bone by bone.

Turn, magic wheel, and force my lover home.

★

How did it start, this misery? Left to myself
I trace the story back to its small beginning.
Eubulus's child, Anaxo, went as altar-girl
To the grove of Artemis. They brought wild animals
And even a lioness for the grand procession.

Think, Lady Moon, how my love came about.

Theumaridas's nurse, the woman from Thrace
Who used to live next door – she's dead and gone now –
Begged me to come and watch the parade. Light-heartedly
I put on my long fine linen dress with the shawl
Clearista lent me, and we set off together.

Think, Lady Moon, how my love came about.

We were half-way along the road, near Lycon's place,
When I saw Delphis walking with Eudamippus.
They had come from the gymnasium, flushed and handsome
After exercise. Their russet beards curled glistening.
Their bare chests shone more splendidly, Moon, than you.

Think, Lady Moon, how my love came about.

In that mad moment my heart burst into flame.
The life went out of my look; I barely noticed
The procession, and how I got myself back home
I don't know. Fever shook me from head to foot.
Ten days and nights I lay helpless on my bed.

Think, Lady Moon, how my love came about.

My skin turned dull and sallow as cinnamon bark.
My hair began to fall out and my body shrank
To skin and bones. I looked everywhere for help,
For a wise woman to charm the sickness away.
I found no relief, and time was hurrying on.

Think, Lady Moon, how my love came about.

At last I spoke to my slave-girl and told the truth:
"Thestylis, you must fetch me the man from Myndus.
He is the whole cause of my sickness; he must cure me.
Wait for him by the wrestling-school of Timagetus.
That's his favourite place for passing the time.

Think, Lady Moon, how my love came about.

'When you see him alone, beckon him over quietly,
Tell him "Simaetha wants you" and bring him here.'
She did as I said and brought him to my house,
Delphis the golden-skinned. When I heard him enter
And the threshold touched by that untroubled step –

Think, Lady Moon, how my love came about –

I froze to a drift of snow; across my forehead
The sweat broke out and ran like a heavy dew.
I could not utter a sound, not even the whimper
A child makes for its mother as it lies asleep.
My body grew stiff as if it were a doll's.

Think, Lady Moon, how my love came about.

Seeing me, he lowered his eyes and sat on the bed.
His words came glibly, full of shallow feeling:
'You beat me to it, Simaetha, only by as much
As I outran young Philinus today on the race-track.
Invited or not, I would have been at your door.

Think, Lady Moon, how my love came about.

'Tonight was the night I meant to come to you,
Bringing two or three good friends for company,
With the apples of Dionysus under my shirt
And on my forehead a garland of white poplar
Sacred to Heracles, twined with purple ribbons.

Think, Lady Moon, how my love came about.

'And well and good if you had taken me in
(Fine-looking and nimble as the young men call me):
One kiss on your lovely mouth and I would have slept.
But if you had pushed me away and bolted the door,
I would have come against you with axes and torches.

Think, Lady Moon, how my love came about.

'Now I offer my thanks to the goddess Cypris
And to you, Simaetha, for coming to my rescue.
Your invitation snatched me out of the fire
Already half-burnt. Love often kindles a blaze
More bright and fierce than Hephaestus on Lipara.

Think, Lady Moon, how my love came about.

'He will draw a bride to leave the still-warm bed
Of her husband, or tempt a young girl from her room,
Scared but wilful...'

                 Full of foolish trust
I reached for his hand and pulled him softly down.
His skin touched mine with secret sudden warmth;
Face to hot face, we murmured. There is no need
To draw out the story, Goddess. What happened happened,
So strange, so commonplace; and both were pleased.
And nothing, no spite or quarrel, came between us
Till yesterday. But this morning, as dawn was breaking
Rosily over the sea, I had a visit
From the mother of Melixo and young Philiste
Our fluteplayer. She told me all her gossip
And among much else, that Delphis was deep in love.
Whether with a man or a woman she couldn't say
But she knew this much: he called for unmixed wine
And drank 'To Love', then hurried off, declaring
That there was a house he must festoon with flowers.
This was what she told me, and she spoke the truth.
He used to come to me three or four times a day
(He kept his oil-flask here for the wrestling-school).
But it's twelve days now since I set eyes on him;
That means he's found a good reason to forget me.
Lucky for him if the magic binds him. If not,
I'll make him beat at death's door to be let in;

There are poisons – strong ones – ready for him in my box;
I brewed them as an Assyrian woman taught me...

Lady, goodbye. Now turn your horses seaward
And leave me to my longing, which I must bear
As I have borne it. Goodbye, remote bright Goddess.
Goodbye, you stars that crowd night's silent path.

3   *The Lovesongs*

I am going to serenade Amaryllis. My goats
Graze on the hill. Tityrus is there to guard them.
Tityrus, do me a favour, look after the goats,
Drive them to water, Tityrus. Watch out for the billy,
The yellow one from Libya, or he will butt you.

★

I am here, Amaryllis. What has become of your love?
Where is the glance that would call me into your cave?

Tell me what fault you found when you saw me close.
Must I hang for a hairy chin or turned-up nose?

I have brought you a gift, ten apples. There, you can see!
Tomorrow I'll bring ten more from your chosen tree.

★

Lucky the bee as it flits through the curtain drawn
Across your cave, dark ivy and maidenhair fern.
O pity my restless heart! Look how I pine!

Now I know Love as he is, an angry god
Suckled by a lioness, reared in a wild wood,
A smouldering fire that burns to the very bone.

The lips may be loving though the heart is unstirred.
Then let yourself be kissed by a clumsy goatherd,
Girl with bright eyes, dark brow and heart of stone.

I am close to breaking point. You will make me tear
This garland (I have kept it for you, my dear)
Where ivy, roses and celery intertwine.

★

What will become of me now? She gives no answer.

Strip this castaway naked and let him fall
From the cliffs where Olpis watches for the tunny shoal.
Then if you are pleased I shall not have died in vain.

To know my fortune I tried the poppy trick,
Smacked down the petal and found it would not stick,
A token of lost love shrivelling on my skin.

All that the wise woman said turns out to be true.
I met her gathering simples and asked about you.
She told me I cared too much and you cared not a pin.

For you I keep a white nanny-goat and her kids,
But I'll do as Mermnon's berry-brown servant bids
And give them to her if you treat me with disdain.

★

My right eye twitched for luck. Shall I see her now?
I shall settle myself against this pine as I sing.
She may take some notice; she isn't made of steel.

★

When bold Hippomenes set his heart on the maid
He took the apples and won the race. Betrayed
By a glance, Atalanta leapt into love's deep lake.

Peiro the gracious lay in the arms of her spouse
When wise Melampus brought back the stolen cows
From Othrys to Pylus, all for his brother's sake.

Adonis the shepherd, feeding his flock on the heath,
Drove Cytherea mad, so that even in death
She cradled him to her breast as if he might wake.

I envy Endymion. May my sleep be as sound
As his. Sweet girl, I envy Iasion bound
On the journey that unillumined ones may not take.

★

My head aches, my legs give way. As if you cared!
No more songs. I shall lie here, food for the wolves.
May you relish that sweetly as honey in your mouth.

4   *The Herdsmen*

BATTUS
Corydon, who do these cows belong to? Philondas?

CORYDON
They're Aegon's herd. He gave me them to graze.

BATTUS
And perhaps at dusk you milk them on the quiet?

CORYDON
The old man watches and brings their calves to suck.

BATTUS
So their master has disappeared! Where's he gone?

CORYDON
To Olympia, with Milon. Didn't you know?

BATTUS
The Games! Since when has he been keen on sport?

CORYDON
They say he's a proper Heracles in the ring.

BATTUS
And I'm a Pollux! or so my mother says.

CORYDON
He went off with his dumb-bells and twenty sheep.

BATTUS
Rabid wolves in the fold would have done less harm.

CORYDON
Listen to the cows lowing. They miss their master.

BATTUS
Poor beasts! The worse for them if he's neglectful.

CORYDON

It's pitiful! They haven't the heart to graze.

BATTUS

There's nothing left of that calf but skin and bones.
Does she breakfast on the dew like a cicada?

CORYDON

Hardly! I sometimes graze her by Aesar's banks
And give her bales of fine soft hay to browse on,
Or else she frisks on Latymnus's shady slopes.

BATTUS

And how lean he is, that tawny bull over there!
A proper victim for the mean-hearted townsfolk
Of Lampriadas, when they sacrifice to Hera.

CORYDON

I drive him to the saltings, to Physcus's place,
To the meadows by Neaethus where plants grow thick,
Restharrow, succory and sweet-smelling balm.

BATTUS

Oh, Aegon! Once you set your heart on the Games
You were on the road to ruin, you and your cows.
The pipe you made for yourself is flecked with mould.

CORYDON

That's safe, at least. When he went off to Pisa
He left it for me as a present. I'm good at piping.
Pyrrhus's tunes and Glauce's quicken at my touch –
'In Croton's fair city', 'Beauty of Zacynthus',
'Sentinel of the morning, Lacinian Shrine…'
There Aegon wolfed eighty barley-cakes at sitting;
There he wrestled with a bull from the hills,
Caught it by the hoof and gave it to Amaryllis.
The women screamed in fright, but he only laughed.

BATTUS

Dear Amaryllis, who can forget your grace?
I think of the loveless, lonely days to come,
And, with you gone, grief stops all other thoughts.

226

CORYDON

Cheer up! Tomorrow shines with its own light.
Living is hoping, Battus. Let the dead despair.
Fine weather or foul, the dawn is always new.

BATTUS

True enough...
               Drive your calves up from below.
Greedy beasts! They're spoiling the olives.

CORYDON

                        Whitey!
Cymaetha! Stir yourselves, get up the bank,
Or I'll come down and give you something to stir for.
She's turning back there. I need a heavy stick,
That's the only language she can understand.

BATTUS

Look here, for god's sake, Corydon! Under my ankle,
A blackthorn spike has run straight in. You see it?
Curse that cow! Like a gaping fool I chased her
Down through the brake and never watched where I trod.

CORYDON

I have the end of it. Gently... there, it's out.

BATTUS

A tiny pinprick, and the whole body quails!

CORYDON

You shouldn't go barefoot on the hillside, Battus.
Wherever you tread, the ground's one thorny ambush.

BATTUS

Tell me, Corydon, is the old man still screwing
That little girl he fancied, the dark-eyed one?

CORYDON

The same as ever. It was only yesterday
Down by the byre that I caught him on the job.

BATTUS

You'll never rest, old boy, till you beat the Satyrs
And thin-shanked Pans at their own horny game.

227

5 Goatherd and Shepherd

COMATAS

Goats, watch out for that shepherd from Sybaris,
Young Lacon! Yesterday he stole my goatskin.

LACON

Get back from the spring, lambs! Don't you see Comatas?
The day before yesterday he took my pipe.

COMATAS

Your pipe! Slave of Sibyrtas, since when have you
Possessed a pipe? Why can't you still be happy
To sit with Corydon, whistling tunes on a straw?

LACON

I beg your pardon! Lycon gave me the pipe;
And that skin you say I took... poor Eumaras,
Your master, doesn't have one to sleep on himself.

COMATAS

I mean the dappled skin that Crocylus gave me
When he offered a goat to the Nymphs. I saw the envy
Filling your eyes. And now you've stripped me bare.

LACON

Pan of the shore be my witness that I, Lacon,
Calaethis's son, never took your cloak. Else let me
Go mad and jump into Crathis from that high rock.

COMATAS

By the Nymphs of the pool, I swear that I, Comatas,
Never laid a finger on your precious pipe:
Else may I never know their grace and favour.

LACON

May I suffer as Daphnis did if I believe you!
But let it go.
            If you're ready to stake a kid
I'll match you, song against song, till you give in.

228

COMATAS

Pigs may whistle though they have an ill mouth for it.
Done! A kid against one of your fattened lambs.

LACON

What kind of bargain is that, you crafty fox?
Who goes to an ass for wool? Who milks a bitch
When a nanny-goat with her firstborn kid stands by?

COMATAS

The clown cocksure of winning before the start,
That's who. But a wasp will buzz at a cicada.
I'll stake you this billy-goat.
                                        Begin the match!

LACON

Gently! You're not on fire. Come and sit down
Under this wild olive; you'll sing more pleasantly.
The trees thin out here. Grasshoppers stitch their music.
A cold stream cuts through the lawn. The turf is soft.

COMATAS

I'm not in a hurry. I'm angry that you dare
To look me straight in the eye. Is this your thanks?
I taught you singing when you were still a boy,
But a snake cherished in the breast will sting the heart.

LACON

If it finds a heart to sting, that is! Remind me,
When did I learn any useful lesson from you?

COMATAS

When I buggered you I taught you to moan and groan
Like a nanny bleating when the billy shoves it in.

LACON

May you be buried no deeper than you can bugger,
Poor cripple!
                    Come over here and sing your last.

COMATAS

I'll stop where I am, among oaks and galingale.
The bees buzz round the hives with friendly warmth.

Cold water gushes from two springs. Birds chatter
From the cover of trees. The tall pine sheds its cones.
The shade's much thicker here than it is with you.

LACON

Choose my ground and you'll tread on lambskin fleeces
Softer than sleep. The goatskins in your shelter
Have an even fouler smell than you do yourself.
I'll set out a basin of fresh white milk for the Nymphs
And beside it another of olive oil, thick and green.

COMATAS

If you join me, you'll tread on pennyroyal
And delicate fern. You'll lie on skins of goats
Four times softer than the lambskins you have there.
I'll set out eight full pails of milk for Pan
And as many saucers of unpressed honeycomb.

LACON

Stay there and sing from the shadow of the oaks
On your own ground.
      Who shall we have as judge?
If only Lycopas the oxherd would come this way.

COMATAS

I wouldn't trust him. But that man over there,
The woodman cutting heather not far from you,
It must be Morson. Give him a shout if you like.

LACON

He'll do.

COMATAS

  You call him.

LACON

    Friend, come over here.
Would you spare us the time to hear our country-songs?
We need a judgement, Morson. I want no favours.
Be certain you're not too kind to him or to me.

COMATAS

Yes, Morson, as you reverence the Nymphs, be fair
To both of us and make sure the best man wins.
That flock belongs to Sibyrtas from Thurii
And these goats here to Eumaras the Sybarite.

LACON

Heavens! Did anyone ask you whether the flock
Was Sibyrtas's or my own? How you love to talk!

COMATAS

It's no more than the truth. Why quarrel with that?
You think I'm getting at you? Don't be so touchy.

LACON

Stop chattering, Comatas. Sing if you can
And let our friend get back to town with his life.

★

COMATAS

The Muses love me more than the singer Daphnis.
I gave them two young goats as a sacrifice.

LACON

And I have Apollo's love. I'm feeding a ram –
When Carnival comes, I'll offer it to him.

COMATAS

All but two of the goats that I milk have twinned.
My girl asks, 'No one to help? I'll lend you a hand.'

LACON

Lacon fills almost twenty baskets with cheeses,
Pulls his boy down among flowers and does what he pleases.

COMATAS

Clearista throws me a quince as I follow my flock.
She pouts her lip and gives me a speaking look.

LACON

Young Cratidas drives his loving shepherd spare.
He stands before me, neck shadowed with bright hair.

COMATAS

The petals of briar and windflower wither and fall,
But the long-lived rose still blooms by the garden wall.

LACON

Acorns or apples, which would you rather eat –
The bitter husk or flesh that tastes honey-sweet?

COMATAS

To please my girl I'll climb up a juniper,
Take a dove from its perch and present it to her.

LACON

That black ewe's fleece will make a handsome coat
For Cratidas. Before he asks, he shall have it.

COMATAS

Move out, my kids, from the oleaster's shadow.
Stay where the hillside steepens and tamarisks grow.

LACON

Conarus, Cinaetha, come out from under the boughs
Of that oaktree; graze in the sun, as Phalarus does.

COMATAS

I have a carved cup and a cypress-wood pail,
Works of a master, treasured up for my girl.

LACON

I have a dog as gentle with sheep as it's fierce
With wolves. My boy shall have it for the chase.

COMATAS

You unwinged locusts that hop over my wall,
The vines are dry there, no good to you at all.

LACON

Look, cicadas, how I vex and fluster him.
He'll get no prey though he smears the reeds with lime.

COMATAS

I hate the vixen with the bushy tail that creeps
Round Micon's place at dusk and steals the grapes.

LACON

And I hate the beetles, carried on the wind,
That nibble Philondas's figs and leave none behind.

COMATAS

Remember the time I bent you over that tree,
How you wriggled, grimaced and pushed back hard on me?

LACON

No. Rather the day when you were stripped and tied
So that Eumaras, your master, could flay your hide.

COMATAS

A charm against anger, Morson! Bring hellebore
From a witch's grave. You see how I've made him sore.

LACON

I've got him ruffled, Morson. Search by the water
For cyclamen bulbs to cure him of his bad temper.

COMATAS

Let Crathis blush with wine, let Himera's spring
Run milk, let reeds bear figs, if I felt the sting.

LACON

At dawn let my girl fill her pail with honeycomb
From the well of Sybaris, if your barbs strike home.

COMATAS

Vetch and clover are my goats' favourite browse.
They walk on mastich and sleep among arbutus.

LACON

Where my sheep graze, rock-roses open around them.
They feed on the starry balsam's fragrant blossom.

COMATAS

I hoped for a kiss when I gave Alcippe a dove.
Alcippe was cool, so I've fallen out of love.

LACON

I love Eumedes. I gave him a set of pipes.
In his delight he kissed me full on the lips.

COMATAS

Swan against hoopoe, nightingale against jay!
However you bluster, Lacon, I'll win the day.

★

MORSON

Stop there, shepherd. Morson awards the lamb
To you, Comatas. Promise you'll send me a handsome
Cut of meat when you sacrifice to the Nymphs.

COMATAS

I promise.
            Now snort me your congratulations,
My flock of kids. Look how I laugh and laugh.
Lacon has lost his lamb, poor foolish shepherd.
I took it from him. O I could leap sky-high.
My horned goats, you've a treat in store. Tomorrow
I'll dip you all in the shallows of Sybaris.
But a word to you, white billy. If you go climbing
On the nannies' backs before I've sacrificed,
I'll break your balls.
                    He's at it again!
                                    If I don't,
Let me pay for it like the goatherd in the story!

6 *Damoetas and Daphnis*

Damoetas and Daphnis had brought their herd together
In the same place, Aratus. The face of one
Was blurred with down, the other had a beard coming.
It was noon in summer. They sat by a spring and sang.
Daphnis began since he was the first to challenge.

★

DAPHNIS

Galatea pelts your flock, Polyphemus, she pelts it
With apples, and calls you goatherd, clumsy lover.
You sit absorbed in the sweetness of your piping
And take not a blind bit of notice. Look now, she aims
At the dog which guards your sheep. It barks in fury
At the wide sea and races its own reflection
Along the foreshore where small waves rustle in.
Call it to heel, or it will dash at her legs
And tear her fine skin when she comes from the sea.
She waits there, teasing you. Like the to-fro drift
Of thistledown as it hangs on the summer air,
If you follow her she flees, if you flee she follows.
She changes the rules as she plays. But often, often
In the game of love, Polyphemus, foul seems fair.

★

Then Damoetas took up the tune and sang a reply:

★

DAMOETAS

I watched her pelting my flock, so help me Pan.
He that has one eye sees the better for it
(Must be afraid to lose it, so Telemus says;
May the wicked prophecy come home to his door).
But I have my game too, and take no notice.
I say her place is filled, and relish the longing
That makes her wild. How sweet her jealousy tastes!
She gazes from the billows at my caves and flocks.
I whistled to my dog to bark. When our love went well,

235

It would whimper and lay its muzzle along her lap.
Let my treatment work on her; she will send a message
Perhaps. But the door is closed till she promises
To share my bed and live with me on this island.
My face is not half so ugly as folk make out.
I studied it just now in a calm sea-hollow,
These handsome cheeks of mine, this handsome eye –
So I honestly thought them; and the water mirrored
My teeth with a whiter gleam than Parian stone.
Then I spat three times on my chest to stop bad luck
As the wise woman Cotyttaris taught me to do.

★

Damoetas closed the song with a kiss for Daphnis,
Gave him his pipe, was given a flute in return.
Then Damoetas began to flute and Daphnis the cowherd
To pipe, while their calves frisked over the soft turf.
There was no winning or losing where both played best.

7   *The Harvest Festival*

Eucritus and I were walking over to Haleis
From town that day. We had taken Amyntas with us.
Demeter was to be given the first-fruits of harvest
By Antigenes and Phrasidamus, Lycopeus's sons,
The best of an old family, Clytia's descendants
And Chalcon's, beneath whose foot the spring Bourina
Welled up as he braced his knee against the rock:
Elms and black poplars make a shady place there,
Its green freshness roofed in by unkempt leaves.
We had not yet gone half-way – the tomb of Brasilas
Was still out of view – when we met another traveller.
The Muses fix such meetings. He was a good man,
A Cydonian called Lycidas; he worked as a goatherd.
You could not mistake him, he so looked the part.
A coarse-haired, shaggy goatskin, the colour of rust,
Smelling of milky rennet, hung from his shoulders.
Beneath lay a threadbare smock, done up with twine
About the waist, and he carried an olivewood crook
In his right hand. He stopped, smiled, challenged me
With friendly eyes and a laugh playing on his lips.
'Simichidas, what are you hurrying for in this heat?
Now even the lizard lies asleep in its cranny
And the tomb-haunting larks have gone to ground.
Are you off to treat yourself at some townsman's winepress
Or to look for a free dinner? What else could stir you
To set the stones singing under those boots of yours?'
I answered him, 'Lycidas, my friend, they tell me
That among herdsmen and harvesters you are the best
At making music. It makes me happy to hear that.
But I have a notion that I might be as good.
Our journey is to a feast, prepared by friends
For Demeter, now that she robes herself in harvest.
They have set aside the first-fruits as an offering
To thank her for a threshing-floor heaped with grain.
But since the road and the day bring us together,
Let's see what we can learn by trying our songs.
I too have been given a clear voice by the Muses;
It has won high praise. But people are easily pleased.
I sing as I can, but nothing of mine yet matches
Sicelidas from Samos or our own Philetas.

237

I compete with them like a frog among cicadas.'
I spoke to tempt him, and with an ingenuous laugh
The goatherd answered, 'Such modesty! You shall have
My crook as a gift for telling god's own truth.
I hate the craftsman who dreams of building his house
As high as the mountain ridge of Oromedon there,
And I hate the artless gaggle of bardic ranters
Who match themselves against Homer with posturing cries.
Now for our songs, Simichidas. I will start
If... But see what you think of this small poem
Which I have been labouring over, up in the hills.'

★

'Let Ageanax have a calm passage to Mytilene
Though Orion sets foot on Ocean's rim, and at dusk
The stormy Kids rise over windswept waves,
If he rescues Lycidas from being burnt alive
By Aphrodite, and answers him love for love.
Halcyons will cast their spell over wind and water,
Quieting the gales which shake the weedstrewn floor.
They are the birds most loved by the green Nereids
And by all who get their living from the sea.
Let Ageanax have fair weather for his voyage
And an easy crossing bring him safe to harbour.
When that day comes I shall place a fragrant garland
– Roses, dill, white stocks – about my head,
And lie by the fire with a bowl of Ptelean wine
To fill my cup from, and a dish of roasted beans.
On my couch, spread elbow-deep with refreshing herbs
– Endive and asphodel and curling parsley –
I shall think of Ageanax with the slow pleasure
Of answered desire as I press my lips to the lees.
I shall have two shepherd pipers, one from Acharnae,
One from Lycope, and Tityrus by me to sing
How Daphnis the cowherd sickened for Xenea's love,
How the hillside shared his pain and how the oaks
By Himera's banks cried his lament, as he wasted
Like a snowfall on the slopes of some high mountain
That lifts its whiteness where we will never climb.
He will sing of the goatherd, how a cruel master
Shut him alive in a chest for his piety,
And snub-faced bees swarmed to the cedar hollow

To feed the prisoner on their meadow-gathered spoil,
Drawn in by the Muse's nectar about his lips.
Lucky Comatas, to take such punishment,
To be shut in a box and fed on honeycomb!
Your pleasant ordeal lasted all one spring.
I wish that you had been living in my day.
I might have watched your goats for you in the hills
And heard your effortless voice, a song from the shade
Of oak or pine where you lay at ease, Comatas.'

★

He finished speaking and I answered, 'Lycidas,
I too have kept a flock in the hills. The Nymphs there
Have made me their pupil and taught me many songs –
How fine they will tell you even in Zeus's court.
Now listen to the poem in which I take most pride,
Sung in your honour since you are the Muses' friend.'

★

'One sneeze from the Loves, and wretched Simichidas
Trots after Myrto, brisk as a goat in spring.
But Aratus, whom I count as my closest friend,
Eats out his heart for a boy. Aristis, the truest
Of singers (jealous Apollo, won by his lyre,
Would welcome him to the sanctuary) knows the secret:
How Aratus is burnt up inside with love for a boy.
Pan, master of Homole's lovely plain, I beg you,
Lay Philinus unresisting in my friend's arms;
Lay him or another there, as gentle to hold.
If you make this happen, dear Pan, the Arcadian boys
Who beat you about the body with rods of squill
When they get no meat, may let you off for once.
But if you refuse, may your bed be nettles, your skin
A mass of bites scratched raw from head to hoof.
May you spend mid-winter in the Edonian mountains
By icy Hebrus, face turned toward the Pole;
May you pasture your flock in an Ethiopian summer
Under the Blemmyan cliff, looking south from Nile.
But leave the clear stream of Hyetis and Byblis,
And leave steep Oecus where blonde Dione presides,
You imps of tender desire, apple-limbed Loves;
Stick Philinus full of arrows despite his beauty,

Stick him with arrows for being unkind to my friend.
Look at him, riper than a plump pear! The women
Cry after him teasingly, 'Philinus, how you have grown!'
We have watched too many nights by his doorstep, Aratus.
Break off the weary patrol. Let it pass to another,
The blank exhaustion when cocks crow up the dawn.
Let your rival, Molon, choke on that wrestling-floor.
Choose peace and quiet. Trust in the wise woman's charm,
A gob of spit to keep off the evil of life.'

★

I finished my song, and with an ingenuous laugh
He gave me the crook, a token of what we had shared.
Then taking the road to the left which leads to Pyxa
He parted from us. Eucritus and I turned off,
With young Amyntas, for Phrasidamus's farm.
There, happy in our welcome, we flung ourselves down
On couches of fragrant reeds and freshcut vineleaves.
Above our heads a grove of elms and poplars
Stirred gently. We could hear the noise of water,
A lively stream running from the cave of the Nymphs.
Sunburnt cicadas, perched in the shadowy thickets,
Kept up their rasping chatter; a distant tree-frog
Muttered harshly as it picked its way among thorns;
Larks and linnets were singing, a dove made moan,
And brown bees loitered, flitting about the springs.
The tall air smelt of summer, it smelt of ripeness.
We lay stretched out in plenty, pears at our feet,
Apples at our sides and plumtrees reaching down,
Branches pulled earthward by the weight of fruit.
The seal broken from the winejars was four years old.
Nymphs of Castalia, haunters of steep Parnassus,
Tell me, was Heracles given such wine to drink
By ancient Chiron in Pholus's rocky cave?
Was it such nectar cheered dull Polyphemus,
The monstrous shepherd who pelted ships with mountains,
To dance on the banks of Anapus among his folds,
As, Nymphs, you mixed for our relishing that day
By the threshing-floor at Demeter's altar?
                                        May I set
The winnowing fan in another year's heaped grain
While the laughing Goddess clutches her poppies and sheaves.

10 *The Reapers*

MILON

Bucaeus, what's the trouble? You're here to work.
You can't cut a swath straight as you used to once;
You don't keep up with the next man, but lag behind
Like a sheep lamed by thorns trailing after the flock.
How will you last till the end of a long day?
It's early yet, but you hardly nibble at the crop.

BUCAEUS

Milon, are you made of flint or flesh and blood?
Have you never felt an absence dishearten you?

MILON

I'm a working man. I keep my mind on the job.

BUCAEUS

Has love never given you a sleepless night?

MILON

Spare me! A hungry dog will eat dirty puddings.

BUCAEUS

For eleven days now, Milon, I've been in love –

MILON

Then you drink a heavy wine, too strong for me.

BUCAEUS

The patch of ground at my door is choked by weeds.

MILON

Who's done this damage?

BUCAEUS

        The girl at Hippocion's farm,
Polybotas's child, who played the flute for the reapers.

MILON

'Take what you want,' God said, 'and pay for it,'
A scrawny insect to cuddle you through the night.

Jeer if you like, but wealth is a blind god too.
If you dream of riches, never laugh at love.

MILON

Don't let your feeling get in the way of your work,
That's all I ask. Put it into a song
While you mow the field. You used to be a singer.

★

BUCAEUS

Muses, sing me a song in praise of my girl.
Everything that you touch you make beautiful.

Bombyca, they call you a gipsy, sunburnt, thin.
I call you slender child with the honey skin.

The violet, the orchid with love-imprinted mark,
The choicest flowers that make up the garland are dark.

The wolf pursues the goat, the goat the clover;
As the ploughshare draws the crane, you draw your lover.

What offering can I make to the sea-born goddess?
– Two golden statues, if I were rich as Croesus:

You with your flute in hand and an apple or rose,
I fitted out in a gentleman's shoes and clothes.

Bombyca, knuckle-bone feet and voice like a flower –
I am lost for words to show how lovely you are.

★

MILON

So Bucaeus is a poet, and we never knew.
What a masterly technique his verse displays!
I belong to the old school, dribbling into my beard,
But the song of Lityerses will bear repeating:

★

Demeter, mother from whom our blessings come,
Look generously on the harvest we bring home.

Binders, bind up the sheaves. Let no man say,
'A wage for the workshy! Good money thrown away!'

The cut end of the swath must look north or west.
When the grain is left lying so, it will ripen best.

Tell the threshers, midday naps are forbidden.
The ear breaks off from the stalk most easily then.

Tell the reapers, you must not wait for the sun.
Rise with the lark, have done when he has done.

Pray for the frog's life, boys. He lives on the brink,
No more than a hop and skip away from his drink.

Boil up the beans, steward. Spice them well for luck.
The seasoning is ill-saved if it shames the cook.

★

That's how men should sing as they work in the sun.
But as for your hungry love, Bucaeus, keep it
For your mother's ears when she wakes you in bed at dawn.

11 *The Cyclops*

I have learnt that there can be no remedy for love,
No special herb or ointment to soothe the heart
Except the Muses. It is light and quick, their drug,
And works for all, but is very hard to find.
I think you know this, Nicias, without my saying,
Since you are doctor and poet, a child of the Nine.
My simple countryman, Polyphemus the Cyclops,
Discovered this long ago when he loved Galatea
And down spread over his cheeks and round his mouth.
His was no game of love-locks and little gifts
But a pure madness that shut out all other thoughts.
His flock would come home to the cave unshepherded
From the green pasture, while he would be off by himself
All day, singing up the dawn on the weedstrewn shore
And pining for Galatea as he nursed the wound
Which the dart from Cypris had cut into his bowels.
Gazing seaward from the high rock where he sat
He found and applied the one remedy.
                                        This was his song:

★

Galatea, why do you treat your lover harshly?
You are whiter than ricotta, gentler than a lamb,
Livelier than a calf, firmer than an unripe grape.
You wait until sleep takes hold of me to come here
And when sleep lets me go, then you slip away
As if you were a sheep and I the great grey wolf.
I fell in love with you, girl, on your first visit.
You came with my mother, wanting to gather orchids
In the hill-meadows. It was I who showed the way.
To you it meant nothing at all. But to me the moment
When I set eyes on you lasts from that day to this.
You slip away from me, girl, unreachably graceful.
No need to say the reason: this shaggy eyebrow
Which stretches from ear to ear across my forehead;
This single eye and flattened nose, these lips.
But fine looks could not buy me the flock I graze,
A thousand strong, nor the milk I draw and drink
Nor the cheese which lasts through summer into autumn

And loads the racks down even to winter's end.
No other Cyclops plays the pipe as I can,
Singing far into the night, my silver pippin,
Of you and me. For your amusement I rear
Four bear-cubs and eleven fawns with dappled coats.
Come to me then. You will never wish yourself back.
Let the green sea waste its anger on the shore:
Night spent in the cave beside me is far more sweet.
Baytrees and slender cypresses grow there, ivy
With its dark leaves and vines with sugary grapes.
Fresh water flows there, which forest-sided Etna
Sends down for me, cold fruit of her white snow.
Who could refuse such things for the cheerless sea?
And if I seem shaggy, I keep in my heart's cave
A fire of oaklogs glowing beneath the cinders.
Let it blaze: I shall not mind how it sears my life
Or shrivels this treasure of treasures, my single eye.
If Mother had only borne me with fish's gills!
I might have dived and found you and kissed your hand
(If you would not give your lips); I might have brought you
Delicate poppies with broad red petals, or snowdrops;
A posy for summer or winter, each in its time.
I could not bring you their white and scarlet together.
I must learn to swim at once; but perhaps if I wait
Some kindly stranger will come in a ship to teach me.
Then I may fathom what pleasure lives in the depths.
Come up from the sea, Galatea. Forget to go home.
I will teach you by my example, sitting here late.
Follow the flocks with me and help me to milk them,
Help me to set the cheese with a dribble of rennet.
Mother is to blame. Though she might have won you
By speaking for me, she said not a single word.
Doesn't she see me grow thinner day by day?
I will tell her my head and feet ache fit to burst,
To make her sicken with worry and suffer like me.
O Cyclops, Cyclops, have you gone out of your mind?
You should be gathering browse to feed your lambs
Or plaiting baskets for cheese; that would show more sense.
Milk the beast you can catch; let the others range.
You will find a new Galatea with lovelier looks.
The girls call after me, 'Shall I see you tonight?'
And laugh in a huddle as soon as I turn my head.
On land, I clearly have something to show for myself.

★

So Polyphemus shepherded his love by singing
And found more relief than if he had paid out gold.

12   *The Touchstone*

You've come, my boy, come after three days' absence
(One day makes a lover old). The difference
Is like that between spring flowers and winter snow,
A fleecy ewe and its lamb, an apple and a sloe,
A fawn and a clumsy calf, a virgin girl
And a three-times-married woman, a nightingale,
Clear-voiced exceller, and all birds besides.
I'm like a traveller at noon whose quickened strides
Bring him to an oak's broad shadow across the path.

If only Love would breathe equally on us both!
Those who come after might put us into a song:
'Once there were words in the old Thessalian tongue
Or the Spartan, for the taking of love and the giving.
These two, long dead, recall for us who are living
The golden time which saw friends honestly paired.
The yoke on their hearts lay light because it was shared.'

Father Zeus and you ageless gods, I pray
That when ten-score generations have had their day
A ghost, new-arrived in the shades, will tell my ghost:
'The story on all lips now, and the young men's most,
Is of you and your companion, adepts in love...'
Whether my wish comes true, let the powers above
Decide as they will. I praise your beauty and worth;
No pimples mark my nose, since I tell no untruth.
You may hurt me a little but, the pain soon past,
The pleasure that follows has a yet keener taste.

Oarsmen of Megara, who make ships your trade,
I wish you happiness for the honour you paid
To Diocles, the hero who died for his friend.
Boys gather about his shrine at winter's end,
Competing to keep his rite. The one who applies
The most skilful lips to give the sweetest kiss
Goes garlanded home to his mother with the prize.
The baffled judge should be happy in his task.
Let him call on bright-faced Ganymede and ask
For a mouth as accurate as the Lydian touchstone
Of moneychangers, by which true gold is known.

13 *Hylas*

When Love, the foundling god, came into our lives
We believed that he existed for us alone.
But, Nicias, how could we think the discovery ours,
Of our day only? We are not the first or last.
Amphitryon's son, whose heart was cased in bronze,
Withstood the savage lion; but he fell for a boy,
For graceful Hylas with long hair still uncut.
He was like a father to the child and taught him
Gently the lessons he had learnt the hard way.
They were never apart. When noon stood in the sky
Or Dawn drove her white horses against the dark,
Or the mother-hen flapped wings on a smoky perch
And made her murmuring chicks look to their roosts,
The example of Heracles was before the boy
So that he might copy and learn how a man lives.
When Jason, the son of Aeson, sailed to recover
The Golden Fleece, and the best men were chosen
From every town to accompany him on the quest,
The hero of many labours, born of Alcmene
Queen of Midea, brought young Hylas with him
To Iolcos; there the good ship Argo lay.
The Black Rocks clashed, but gliding through unscathed
She swept like an eagle into the soundless gulf
Of Phasis: since that day the crags stand fixed.

When the Pleiads rise and signs of summer thicken
And lambs are put to graze in the upland meadows,
The band of heroes grew restless for their voyage:
They took their places in hollow Argo, set sail
For the Hellespont and three days' fair wind brought them
To anchor in Propontis, by the land of Cius
Where cattle labour at the bright-bladed plough.
They disembarked and prepared the evening meal,
Sitting in groups; but first they cut their bedding
In a near-by meadow and made one mattress for all:
The fleshy stalks of galingale spread with rushes.
Hylas had gone off, yellow-haired through the dusk,
A bronze vessel in his hands to bring back water
For the dinner which Heracles and fierce Telamon
Would eat together, as usual. He found a pool

In a valley hollow, plants growing thick about it,
Green maidenhair, marsh-creeping dog's-tooth grass,
Wild celery, rich celandines, tall flags.
There the Nymphs trod an underwater dance
– Unresting presences, feared the country round –
Eunica, Malis, Nycheia with spring in her eyes.
The boy leant down and forced the vessel's mouth
Beneath the surface; they grabbed his hand, they pulled,
Their clear thoughts shocked and scattered by desire
For the young stranger.
                        He toppled into the darkness,
Toppled like a star that shoots from sky to sea
Bright, sheer and gone; while sailor calls to sailor,
'Loosen the tackle, lads. There's a wind blowing up.'
Hylas struggled and wept but they stretched his body
Across their knees and whispered to reassure him.
Amphitryon's son grew alarmed at the boy's absence.
He took up his springy Scythian bow and the club
Which he carried in his right hand, and went off to look.
'Hylas', he bellowed three throat-wrenching cries.
Each time the boy replied; but his voice came faint
From the pool, as if he were calling from a distance.
Like a mountain lion when it hears a whimpering fawn
And bounds from hiding to make a meal of the prey,
Heracles tore through thorny brakes in an anguish
Of worry; he searched the hillsides, searched the forests,
Punishing himself as lovers do when their hope
Has failed. The voyage with Jason was clean forgotten.
Next day the ship stood ready, her tackle raised
And her crew in place. The heroes took down the sails
As they waited for Heracles; but he wandered blindly,
Maddened by the enemy, by the god in his heart.

Now Hylas lives, unfading, among the Immortals.
The heroes taunted Heracles as a deserter.
Not so: he finished the journey, and came on foot
To the land of the Colchians and unwelcoming Phasis.

14 *Aeschines and Thyonichus*

AESCHINES

Good to see you, Thyonichus.

THYONICHUS
        And you, Aeschines.

It's been some time.

AESCHINES
    It has.

THYONICHUS
    What's up with you?

AESCHINES

Trouble, Thyonichus.

THYONICHUS
    Look how thin you've got;

Unshaved moustache, long straggly hair! You're like
That pasty-faced barefoot 'philosopher'
Who came by the other day. 'From Athens,' he said.

AESCHINES

Was he in love too?

THYONICHUS
    Pining... for a square meal.

AESCHINES

You can joke! It's driven me nearly crazy,
The way Cynisca's been messing me about.

THYONICHUS

You could never take things easy, Aeschines.
You want everything 'just right'...
              Tell me the worst.

AESCHINES

The Argive and Agis, the trainer from Thessaly,
And me and the soldier, Cleunicus – we were drinking

At my country place. I'd killed a sucking pig
And a pair of chickens, opened a jar of old wine
– It smelt as good, almost, as the day it was pressed –
Got onions and snails. It was a proper party.
When things were going nicely we offered a toast
'To the one I love', and we had to say the name.
We all spoke up and the toast went round. But *she*
Went quiet. And me right there! You can guess my feelings.
'Seen a wolf?' quipped someone. 'That's right,' she said,
Then blushed. You could have lit a lamp at her cheeks.
There is a wolf – a wolf at the door, you might say.
My neighbour Labas's son. That's her great lover!
Handsome they call him. Skinny and overgrown!
A whisper about it had reached my ears, it's true,
But I took no notice. Trusting as a babe, I was.
Well, the four of us had had a few by this time,
And the man from Thessaly sang 'Little Red Ridinghood'
Right through from the beginning, which didn't help.
Cynisca burst into tears like a girl of six
Sobbing to be taken up on her mother's lap.
So I let her have it, Thyonichus – you know me –
I smacked her about the head a couple of times,
'Not good enough for you, am I?' She picked herself up
And ran. 'Don't hang around, dear. That boyfriend of yours
Will be catching cold. I hope he makes you cry.'
A swallow, bringing a scrap to its young in the eaves,
Darts out a split-second later to fetch more food:
That's how she was, one moment stretched in a chair,
The next, flying down the passage and out of the house.
Talk about the stable door and the bolting horse!
Twenty days... then eight... nine... then ten more...
Eleven till today. Plus two makes two whole months
Since we split up. If I spiked my hair like a Thracian
She'd never notice the change. The Wolf's her man now,
She has him in at nights.
                                        I'm out in the cold,
No room for a poor Yahoo like me in her life.
If I could stop thinking about her, well and good.
But as it is... I'm like a mouse in a trap.
What the doctor orders to treat a lover's pangs
I don't know. But when my old friend Simus fell
For that brassy girl, a sea-voyage did the trick.
I'll cross the sea too, and enlist as a soldier –

Not the best life, perhaps, but it could be worse.

THYONICHUS

I only wish that things had gone as you wanted,
Aeschines. But if serving abroad's your answer,
King Ptolemy gives a free man honest terms.

AESCHINES

Tell me more.

THYONICHUS

Ptolemy's one of the best!
Warm-hearted, loves his mistresses, loves learning,
Never forgets a friend – or an enemy.
He's generous to a fault, as a great prince should be,
But be careful not to push your luck in asking,
Aeschines. If you're ready to sling a soldier's
Cloak about your shoulders and bear the brunt
Of an enemy charge without budging from your place,
Hurry to Egypt.
                        A touch of grey at the temples
Creeps outward, hair by hair, and before we know it
Our time has gone. Act now, while the sap runs green.

15   *The Festival of Adonis*

(Praxinoa's house, a suburb of Alexandria)

GORGO

Is Praxinoa home?

PRAXINOA

Gorgo, at last! My dear!
I'd almost given up hope of seeing you here.
(*to slave*)
Eunoa, a chair and a cushion.

GORGO

That's fine.

PRAXINOA

Sit down.

GORGO

I'm quite exhausted. I hardly got across town
Alive, Praxinoa. The people! The chariots!
Everywhere, men in cloaks and hobnailed boots.
The road seems longer each time I call on you.

PRAXINOA

Blame my mad husband for that. What wouldn't he do –
Live in a hovel or move to the world's end,
Selfish bugger! – to cut me off from a friend?

GORGO

Your Dinon has his faults, but we shouldn't chatter
In front of the child. He's staring!
(*to the child*)
What's the matter,
Zopyrion, my duck! It's not Daddy we mean.

PRAXINOA

Bless us! The little one's taking it all in.

GORGO

Lovely Daddy!

PRAXINOA

Lovely indeed! When I told him
To buy some bath-salts, you know what the shopman sold him?
Cooking-salt. The great fool! No wonder I scold him.

GORGO

Diocleidas is just the same, throws money away.
You should see the fleeces he bought yesterday,
Five of them, mangy, thick with dirt. And the price!
What a job they'll be...
                              Now make yourself look nice.
We're going out. The show the Queen's putting on is
The finest yet, I've heard, *The Masque of Adonis*.
In Ptolemy's palace too. What a place to visit!

PRAXINOA

Nothing but the best for her.

GORGO

                              A pity to miss it.
Change into your summer dress. It's time we were going.

PRAXINOA

Idle folk lack no excuses.
                              (to the slave)
                              Eunoa, the sewing!
The cats are sure to curl up on it. Put it away.
Quickly, bring me some water. – Water, I say,
And she gives me the soap! Will nothing go right today?
No leave it here now. Clumsy! You've splashed my blouse.
Pour gently. There, I'm as clean as heaven allows.
Fetch me the key to the clothes-chest. Do as you're told!

GORGO

Praxinoa, I like the full dress with the fold.
It suits you perfectly. What did you pay for the stuff?

PRAXINOA

Two pounds in silver, Gorgo. More than enough.
I worked my heart out embroidering the pattern.

GORGO

It couldn't have turned out better, that's for certain.

PRAXINOA

(to the slave)
My hat and shawl now. Carefully!

                      Zoppy, my pet,
You're to stay at home. It's no good getting upset.
The horsey'll bite. You'll be under everyone's feet.
Here, Phrygia, you take baby and keep him amused.
Call the dog in and see that the front-door's closed.

                   ★

(The streets of Alexandria)

PRAXINOA

How shall we manage to find our way through this mob?
I've never known it so packed. It's a proper job
King Ptolemy's cleaned things up since his father died.
Wherever you turned, some Gypsy was at your side
To rob you if you gave him a chance, in the past –
Pickers and stealers, each one as bad as the last.
If we were ants in an antheap, it couldn't be worse.
Gorgo, watch out! If it's not a man it's a horse.
The cavalry of the King!

                     Get off my feet, sir!
That chestnut stallion's rearing, the crazy creature.
Eunoa, don't you go near. He'll trample his groom.
Thank heavens I left the baby safely at home!

GORGO

All clear, Praxinoa. They've gone to their places,
A long way off.

PRAXINOA

               I've never liked snakes or horses
Since I was a child. Ugh! But I'm quick to recover.
We'd better go with the crowd or they'll push us over.

GORGO

(to an old woman)
Are you from the palace, mother?

OLD WOMAN

                   I am, my dears.

GORGO

Is it easy to get in there?

OLD WOMAN
                    Greeks spent ten years
Getting into Troy. You won't have to wait so long.

GORGO

Riddles and proverbs!

PRAXINOA
                    If old women knew what song
The Sirens sang, they'd never tell it you straight.

GORGO

Praxinoa, look how they're crowding in at the gate.

PRAXINOA

Take my hand, Gorgo. Eunoa, take the hand
Of Eutychis. Hold it tight. Do you understand?
We must go in together. Don't get left behind.
Careful! Perhaps this gentleman here would mind
Not pulling against my wrap, if he can't keep steady.
Just my luck! It's torn down the middle already.

MAN

I'm doing my best. I'm caught like you in the crush.

PRAXINOA

They jostle like pigs.

MAN
                    Keep going now. One more push!

PRAXINOA

Without you, sir, I don't know where we'd have been.
You deserve a medal for getting us safely in.
They're smothering Eunoa.
                    (to the slave)
                    Shove, or you'll stay outside!
'All in', as the man said, turning the key on his bride.

(In the palace precinct)

GORGO

Come here, Praxinoa. Look at the tapestries.
So prettily finished! Robes that the gods would prize.

PRAXINOA

Gracious Athene! I can hardly believe my eyes.
Such cloths! They're never the work of human hands.
Look at the artists' figures. Here's one that stands
Getting his breath back, another that seems to move.
And there's Adonis, our handsome prince of love,
Lolling on his silver chair, cheeks touched with down –
Adonis, our darling on earth and in Acheron.

SECOND MAN

Quiet, women! Chattering like two barn-door fowls.
You set my teeth on edge with your flattened vowels.

PRAXINOA

What bird might you be? The crested ignoramus?
We come of good Corinthian stock, the same as
Bellerophon. We're women from Syracuse, famous
For our quick tongues, and we're proud of how we speak.
Who dares say we Dorians don't talk proper Greek?
There's only one man interferes in my life
And that's not you, sir. Save your breath for your wife.

GORGO

Shh, Praxinoa, shh! The singer's come on,
The Argive woman's girl. You remember she won
The prize last year? She's a mistress of her art.
She's cleared her throat. That means she's about to start.

★

SINGER

Queen Aphrodite, leave your chosen home,
Golgi, Idalium or steep Eryx. Come,
Goddess of gilded play, attend your feast.
The Hours, soft-footed, slowest of the Blessed
(And how impatiently we wait for them!)

Bring back Adonis over Acheron's stream.
Lady of Cyprian fields, Dione's child,
Whom Berenice thanks for godhead, filled
Along her mortal veins with heavenly food:
See how Arsinoë gathers all that's good
To lull Adonis, for whose love you pined
Yearlong, O many-named and many-shrined.
Beside him golden pots of myrrh are placed
And fruit fresh from the tree, the season's best;
Mouth-watering dishes; every kind of meat,
Elaborate cakes and puddings, moist and sweet;
The world of fancies pastry-cooks devise
From honey and oil and coloured essences.
Green canopies of branches spread above,
Where childish figures of the God of Love
Open their wings like fledgling nightingales.
Miniature gardens, fenced with silver pales,
Are planted out; and dill perfumes the air.
O splendours of the couch! Carved eagles bear
An ivory Ganymede through golden sky,
And soft as sleep the purple blankets lie.
Let Samos and Miletus say with pride,
'Our looms have served Adonis and his bride.'
Eighteen years young! the down still on his face,
He holds the goddess in a flushed embrace,
As she holds him and kisses his smooth lips.
Soon, Aphrodite, comes your joy's eclipse!
At dawn, before the dew fades from the ground,
Your lover must be carried out and drowned:
We'll float him seaward, singing our lament
With loosened hair, breasts bared and garments rent.
Half-god, half-man! Adonis, you alone
Cross back to this world over Acheron.
Not Hector, the firstborn of twenty sons,
Not Neoptolemus, Troy's victor once,
Not Agamemnon, has achieved such grace;
Nor the ancient Lapiths nor Deucalion's race.
Patroclus and harsh Ajax lie below
With the Pelasgian kings. But you bestow
Your presence on us, year by year, and bless us now.

★

Praxinoa, what wouldn't I give to sing like that!
Time to go home. Diocleidas will be in a state.
It's more than my life's worth if his dinner's late.
Goodbye, Adonis. I pray that you find us here,
Healthy and happy, when you come back next year.

16 *The Graces*

The proper task of Zeus's daughters and of poets
Is to celebrate the gods and great men's lives.
The Muses are heavenly beings; they sing of heaven.
We are earthbound creatures; we too should sing our own.

Where does he live, beneath what glittering sky,
The man who will open his house to receive our Graces,
Not turn them away unrecognized, unrewarded?
They come home sulky, trailing their bare feet
And blame me for sending them on a wasted journey;
Then they crouch at the bottom of a wooden coffer,
Their heads on their cold knees, their confidence gone.
Where can they turn, when every door is closed?
Show me the man with a proper sense of glory,
Who knows the praiser's worth. Can he still be found?
Now the cry is, 'Give me the money, keep the praise',
And each man cradles silver under his shirt,
Jealous even of its tarnish, with greed in his eyes
And a smug rebuff on his lips: 'It's all in Homer';
'The gods will look after the poets – that's their job';
'Charity begins at home' – and goes no further;
'The poet I like is the one who costs me nothing'.

But, gentlemen, how does it help you to lock away
Your wealth? A wise man, putting his money to use,
Takes care of himself, but does not forget the poet.
A crowd of dependants and family count on his help;
He provides the altars with offerings for the gods;
He welcomes guests to his table, a generous host,
And sends them away cheered when they choose to leave;
But the Muses' servants receive his special care.
That way you shall be rewarded when death hides you,
Not loiter by cold Acheron, shorn of your fame,
No better than a poor labourer with callused hands
Who swings a mattock and hoards a birthright of tears.
In the halls of Antiochus and kingly Aleuas
An army of bondsmen gathered for the monthly dole;
At nightfall the pens of the Scopadae were crowded
With wide-horned cattle lowing to meet their young;
The shepherds who served the hospitable Creondae

Ranged Crannon's open ground with numberless flocks:
All joy of possession vanished when once their souls
Were emptied into the sour old ferryman's barge
And they went down into darkness with the common ghosts,
Severed from their fortunes; they would be clean forgotten
If the subtle music and bright-emblazoning voice
Of the Cean poet had not named and made them known
In times to come. We remember even their horses,
Honoured creatures who brought them prizes from the games.
What would they mean to us, Cycnus with womanly skin
Or the Lycian chiefs or Priam's long-haired sons,
If poetry did not ring with their ancient war-cries?
Or Odysseus? For ten years he wandered the wide world;
He came alive to Hades, he entered the cave
Of the deadly Cyclops and lived to tell the tale,
While Eumaeus watched the pigs and Philoetius the cows
And noble Laertes tended his patch of ground:
Great names, but they would have vanished all alike
If the blind Ionian had not come to their rescue.

Though living men make free with a dead man's goods,
The Muses' gift of fame can never be taken.
But to sit and count the waves which wind and sea
Drive shoreward in grey succession, or fetch clear water
To wash a mudbrick clean, is the game of a fool;
And you will as soon heal a miser's damaged heart.
Goodbye to the miser! Let him keep his silver;
With all his useless wealth, let him pine for more.
I think goodwill and honour are truer possessions
Than the mules and horses in a rich man's stable.
I look for a patron eager to take me in,
And the Muses with me. The roads are not safe for poets
Unless wise Zeus's daughters are there to guide them.
Untiringly heaven brings the months and years;
The horses stir, and day's bright wheel lifts high:
I will find the Achilles, the Ajax of our age,
And celebrate exploits great as those performed
Where Simois runs by the tomb of Phrygian Ilus.
Now the Phoenicians, dwellers on the hot shore
Of Africa, shiver with fear; their sun sinks low.
The men of Syracuse grip their spears for battle,
They shoulder their heavy wicker shields; among them
Hiero stands, armed and ready, a pattern of valour,

His gleaming helmet shadowed by a horsehair crest.

I beg you, Father Zeus and Lady Athena,
And you who watch over Syracuse, the great city
By the Lake of Lysimeleia, you and your mother:
Let violence clear our enemies from this island,
Allowing a handful only to sail back home
To bring their women and children news of slaughter.
May the old inhabitants repossess their cities,
Build on ruins and restore what has been spoiled.
May the fields be worked and bring forth crops once more
While bleating flocks, too many to count, grow fat
On the grassy plains. May the passer-by at nightfall
Quicken his steps as the cattle are driven home.
Let fallows be ploughed for sowing while the cicada,
The shepherd's sentinel, high among branches, rasps
The midday silence. Let the armoury be shrouded
In cobwebs, the war-cry become a forgotten sound.
Let poetry carry Hiero's fame through the world
From Scythian waters to where the asphalt rampart
Raised by Semiramis guards her ancient kingdom.
I am one among many poets, each with a claim
On the Muses, each ready to celebrate Arethusa,
Her brave Sicilians and Hiero, lord of the spear.
O Gracious Goddesses, worshipped by Eteocles,
Who love Orchomenus, Thebes's once loathed rival,
I will not jostle for notice but, if summoned,
Will answer gratefully, gladly – I and my Muses.
You too must accompany me. There is no delight
When once the Graces have gone. Let me not betray them.

17 *Encomium to Ptolemy*

Zeus is the first of gods and has first claim.
My poem begins and ends with Zeus's name,
But turns for the remainder of its span
To Ptolemy, since he's the noblest man.
The sons of demigods in ancient days
Found poets worthy to rehearse their praise.
I take a king, the best of kings, for theme.
Song is a gift which even gods esteem.
A forester on Ida gazes round,
In doubt where first to clear a patch of ground:
I pause among the favours heaven bestows
On Ptolemy, unsure which first to choose.

With forbears I'll begin; with Lagus' son,
Old Ptolemy, dreamer and doer, one
Who'd carry through what others would not even
Dare to conceive. Zeus gathered him to heaven,
The father to the Father. A gold throne
Set for him near his old companion,
Bright-diademed Alexander, bane of the East,
He sits among the gods and shares their feast.
The Centaur-killer, mighty Heracles
Sits opposite, enthroned on steel, and sees
(Joy touching his stern heart) his progeny
Transformed to gods, healed of mortality
By Cronus' son, their stock proclaimed divine.
To Heracles both kings trace back their line
And in his valiant son unite their stem.
He rises from the feast and hands to them
His club, blunt-ridged with iron, his shafts and bow.
They bear his arms before him as they go,
Proud to escort a god, born of a god,
Amorous with nectar, to his wife's abode,
To shining-ankled Hebe's fragrant house.

Of virtuous women the most virtuous,
Her parents' pride, how Berenice shone!
Your hands, child of Dione, once laid on
Imparted to her limbs a Cyprian touch.
They say no woman pleased her man as much.

Ptolemy loved, and yet she loved him more.
With such a wife a husband may be sure
That both his property and native worth
Are blamelessly passed on when she gives birth.
An untrue wife resists her man's embrace;
The child she bears him has a stranger's face.
Queen Aphrodite, heaven's bright paragon,
You rescued Berenice. Acheron
Remained uncrossed; hell lay unvisited.
The surly boatman who conveys the dead
In his dark barge never appalled her sight.
She shares your temple, shares your holy rite,
Bringing love's gentlest gift to humankind,
Desire that quickens and yet soothes the mind.
The dark-browed Argive bore a murderous son,
Diomede, to Tydeus, prince of Calydon.
Deep Thetis bore Achilles, bold in war,
To Peleus. Noble Berenice bore
You, Ptolemy, a warrior king by race,
To Ptolemy; and Cos, the proud birth-place,
Received you to be nursed on that first day.
In childbed there Antigone's daughter lay
Calling Ilithyia to ease her throes.
The goddess came, stood by and shed repose
On her tense limbs. Gently the longed-for boy
Was born, his father's image. Filled with joy,
Cos cradled him in her fond arms, crying out,
'God bless you! May the fame Apollo brought
To sea-encircled Delos now be mine.
Be no less gracious to the hilltop shrine
Of Triopos and the Dorian League, my kin,
Than Phoebus to Rhenaea, Delos' twin.'
Zeus answered with a sign. Sheer through the sky
An eagle swept and with its triple cry
Thrilled the cloudrack, soaring on fateful wings.
Zeus, the preserver of illustrious kings,
Grants to his favourites whom he loves from birth
Treasure and empire for their lot on earth.
Through the whole world men born to plough and sow
Look to wet skies to make their harvests grow.
Only in Egypt, where the enormous plain
Is soaked by flooding Nile, crops need no rain.
Each fattened acre boasts its husbandry.

You'd count the cities? Multiply by three
Eleven thousand, add three hundred more,
Thirty, then three, to reckon up the score.
All these acknowledge Ptolemy's command.
Syria, Phoenicia, Libya yield their land.
Arab and black-skinned Ethiop feel his sword.
Lycia, Pamphylia, Caria call him lord,
Lord fierce Cilicia, sea-washed Cyclades.
His ships proclaim him sovereign of the seas.
Through both empires, the watery and the dry,
All power begins and ends in Ptolemy;
He stands among his soldiers, troops of horse
And steel-bright foot, the veterans of his wars.

His wealth outweighs all wealth of other kings,
Still growing with the tribute each day brings
From every side. In peace men till the soil.
No nimble raiders leap ashore to spoil
Egyptian pastures of their herds, nor dare
Cross Nile's beast-haunted boundary to scare
Quiet homesteads with an alien battle-cry.
So strong a king as fair-haired Ptolemy
Is throned in these broad plains and, great in arms,
Secures his father's territory from harms –
A realm which his own conquests overtop.
His treasure's put to use, not huddled up
In miserly restraint like the poor hoards
Amassed by ants. The temples of the gods
Take the first-fruits, their portion and to spare.
Cities and vassal kings are given a share.
His brave companions too receive a part.
No clear-voiced singer, practising his art
In Dionysus' honour, lacks reward.
Proudly the servants of the Muse record
Their patron's bounty and exalt his name,
Ptolemy the Generous! What nobler aim
Can wealth achieve than honour in the world?
The Atridae keep their fame. But all their gold
Taken at Troy, however bright it shone,
Lies swallowed up in dark oblivion.

Uniquely among men of former days
And men whose warm tracks mark the dusty ways,

Ptolemy has built shrines with pious care,
Proclaimed his parents gods and placed them there,
Chryselephantine forms, as mankind's friends.
On their fired altars as each season ends
He and his consort burn fat oxen's thighs;
She partners him in filial sacrifice.
In her embraces he delights to find
Two loves, a sister's and a wife's, combined.
Such holy wedlock binds Queen Rhea's children.
Let none dispute a marriage made in heaven,
Where virginal Iris' fragrant hands prepare
The single couch which Zeus and Hera share.

Goodbye, Lord Ptolemy. Thanks to my Muse,
The time to come will rank your name with those
Of gods and heroes. But for virtue pray to Zeus.

18 *Helen's Epithalamium*

Sparta. The mansion of yellow-haired Menelaus.
Twelve young girls, the city's strength and pride,
Assemble, with hyacinths in their hair, to dance
In front of the newly painted marriage-chamber.
The doors are fastened. The younger son of Atreus
Has taken Helen, Tyndareus's child, to wife.
They beat time on the floor with intricate steps
And chant a bridal song. The whole house echoes.

★

So soon asleep? Bridegroom, your drowsy head
And heavy limbs disgrace the marriage-bed.
If you're the worse for drink, send back your bride.
She'll find more comfort at her mother's side,
Drawing out the hours till late in girlish play.
Sleep by yourself. Spare her for one more day.
You can afford to, since she's yours for good.
Some lucky star marked you among the crowd
Of Grecian lords bidding for Helen's hand.
You've won her now, the beauty of our land,
Zeus's daughter, to share your bed. No other
Hero can claim a wife with such a father.
She'll bear a fine child if it's like its mother!

Girls though we are, we love to swim and run,
To strip and smear ourselves with oil. But none
Who gathers by Eurotas for our sport
Dares match herself with Helen. Each falls short.
Lovely after the night the rising dawn.
Lovely the whitening spring when winter's gone.
So Helen shines, golden among her peers.
A trace-bound filly, a cypress tree that rears
Its dark adornment over field and garden,
Helen, the rose-flushed, graces Lacedaemon.
None, seated at the loom, is half so deft
As she with yarn and shuttle, or cuts a weft
More finely woven from the crossbar strings.
When Helen strikes the hollow lyre and sings,
Her praise is of the virgin deities;

While Aphrodite signals from her eyes.

Your title now is wife. Girlhood, farewell!
We'll miss you, Helen, like young lambs that kneel
To butt their mother's belly for the teat.
Early tomorrow, by the Course, we'll meet
And search the unmown fields for flowers to weave
Into sweet-smelling garlands. One we'll leave
Beneath a plane-tree's shade, of low trefoil;
Beneath a plane-tree's shade we'll pour out oil
From silver flasks – the first to keep your rite –
And cut in bark, where passers-by can see it,
This legend, 'Worship me. I am Helen's tree.'

Now goodbye to you, bride! Bridegroom, goodbye!
May both be gainers in love's give and take,
And healthy children bless the love you make.
May the great wealth Heaven grants to you and yours
Still gladden those who'll call you ancestors.
Let passion and desire, as sleep comes on,
Mingle your breaths. Be sure you wake at dawn.
When the cock lifts his glittering neck to crow
We'll come again.
                    It's time to leave you now.
Hymen, approach and bless this couple's marriage-vow.

22   *The Dioscuri*

A hymn for the children whom Leda bore to Zeus,
Lord of the aegis – Castor and his fierce brother,
Pollux, who straps his palms with oxhide thongs.
A hymn, twice over and again, for the boys
Born in Lacedaemon to Thestius's daughter:
Rescuers of men whose lives hang in the balance,
Of horses panicked in battle's bloody turmoil,
Of ships which put out to challenge the constellations
Rising or setting, and run into dangerous storms.
Then winds heap up the water till a swamping wave
At stern or prow or side comes riding over
And crashes full into the hold. The bulwarks crack,
The sail flaps tattered, the broken tackle swings.
Night falls. The rain intensifies, sheet on sheet,
Driving over the broad sea, which heaves and roars
Beaten by the thudding air and scored with hail.
You pull ships clear as the gulf closes above them
When every sailor is sure that he must perish:
In a moment the wind has fallen, the sea-surface
Lies calm and sleek, the cloud-cover melts away.
The stars of the Bear shine out, the Asses' Manger
Flickers its sign, and all's set fair for the voyage.
You, the twin helpers of men on earth, excellers
In words and music, on horseback, at the games,
Castor and Pollux, whom shall I celebrate first?
Let Pollux open the hymn, where both are honoured.

★

The Rocks rushed inward. Argo kept her course.
Too late the freezing Euxine shut its jaws
Against the chiefs and demigods who manned
The first of ships. They brought her into land –
Sheltered Bebrycia where the beach lay wide.
Out went the ladders; down the vessel's side
They climbed, to heap up beds and set fires burning.
Castor and Pollux left their friends and, turning
Inland, set off to climb the nearby hill.
They searched its wilderness of woods until
They found a pool. Beyond, the cliff rose sheer

269

And from its hollow base throughout the year
Springwater welled, plentiful, cold and clear
Over bright pebbles. Close around grew trees,
Tall pines, planes, poplars, slender cypresses,
Wild flowers whose scent through the last days of spring
Drew down the bees to endless harvesting.
An ogrish figure sat there in the sun:
His chest and back gleamed as if made of iron,
The sculpted flesh still bulging in repose;
His features blunt, his ears thickened with blows.
Along his brawny arms and jutting shoulders
The muscles ran in coils, like heavy boulders
Strewn by a winter torrent in its course,
All tumbled smooth. A lionskin, tied by the paws,
Hung down its shaggy splendour from his neck.
Pollux approached him and made bold to speak:

POLLUX
Stranger, good day. What men live in this place?

AMYCUS
Here no day's good that brings a foreign face.

POLLUX
Don't be afraid. We've come to do no harm.

AMYCUS
Do I look like the sort who takes alarm?

POLLUX
Why this ill-natured talk? Be friendlier!

AMYCUS
Ill-natured, yes. But I'm no trespasser.

POLLUX
We welcome guests and treat them generously.

AMYCUS
I'll take no gifts and you'll get none from me.

POLLUX
You'll give us leave at least to quench our thirst!

AMYCUS

One sip of water and you'll learn the worst.

POLLUX

If words or gifts can't win you, say what can.

AMYCUS

Put up your fists and face me, man to man.

POLLUX

Boxing or wrestling? Name what rules you will.

AMYCUS

Boxing. Be sure you fight with all your skill.

POLLUX

Then say who fights me, hand to thong-bound hand.

AMYCUS

The Champion. See how strong and close I stand.

POLLUX

We need a prize. What shall the winner have?

AMYCUS

His beaten adversary, to be his slave.

POLLUX

Bright-crested gamecocks fight on terms like these.

AMYCUS

Like gamecocks then, or lions, or what you please,
We'll stake ourselves. Hope for no other prize.

Amycus raised his conch and blew a blast.
The long-haired Bebryces came swarming fast
Out of the woods, and gathered in the shade
Of the broad planetrees. Castor, unafraid,
Went back and called the heroes from the ship.
The antagonists prepared: a hardened strip
Of oxhide bound about each arm and hand,
They came out, breathing hard, and took their stand.
Each circled, struggling for the better place,

To have the sun shine full in the other's face.
Your skill, Tyndareus' son, outpaced his size.
Then Amycus, who stood with dazzled eyes,
Lunged forward, angry that he could not win
The advantage. Swarthy Pollux caught his chin
With a sharp blow. But still the giant came on
With scattered wits and random swipes, head down
And fighting mad. The Bebryces roared out,
'Kill him!' The heroes countered with a shout,
'Don't let him crowd you. Give yourself more room!'
Scared that sheer plodding bulk might overcome
Their nimble champion. Fist on cutting fist,
This way and that he darted, to resist
Poseidon's son and break his vast attack.
Punch-drunk and spitting blood, the giant stood back.
The heroes' warning cries turned to applause:
They saw dark cuts about his mouth and jaws
And how his face swelled, so that he looked out
Through narrow slits. Now, to complete the rout,
Pollux came at him fast with feinted blows,
Then struck his forehead, full above the nose,
Landing a punch that skinned the bony mass
And sent him sprawling hugely in the grass.
He staggered to his feet. Again the grim
Debate of blunt-thonged fists with life and limb
Began. Amycus rallied, but at best
The blows glanced off his rival's neck and chest.
His face became one bruise, his flesh fell in,
And as the melting sweat streamed down his skin
His gianthood shrank till he stood poor and slight,
While clear-skinned Pollux drew strength from the fight.

Assist your spokesman, Goddess! Tell me how
This savage chieftain met his overthrow.
Knowledge is yours to give. Say what you'd have us know.
'It's all or nothing now,' Amycus thought.
Dropping his guard, he leant across and caught
Pollux by the left arm, forced back the wrist,
Stepped suddenly close and brought up his right fist.
Then old Amyclae might have lost its king,
But, ducking sideways, Pollux took a swing
At the left temple of the sea-god's son,
Burst it, and sent the black blood gushing down.

A smart blow to his mouth (the left arm freed)
Followed by a rain of punches to his head:
Dizzy, with rubbished face and rattling teeth,
Amycus tottered, fell, lay close to death,
Both hands stretched out disclaiming further fight.
The victory yours, Pollux, you worked no spite
On him, though fallen. His forfeit was to swear
An oath to Poseidon that he would not dare
Molest another stranger making landfall there.

★

You have your place now, Prince. I turn to your brother,
Spearman and horseman, lord of the brazen corselet.

★

The story goes that the two heaven-born ones
Kidnapped the girls betrothed to Aphareus' sons,
Cheating Lynceus and Idas of their suit.
The would-be bridegrooms, driving in pursuit,
Waylaid the kidnappers and checked their flight.
They all sprang down by Aphareus' tomb to fight,
Clutching their heavy shields, their spears and swords.
First Lynceus spoke these helmet-muffled words:
'Why must we come to blows? How can you deal
In broken promises? Does naked steel
Make good false claims? Bound by their father's oath
Sworn long ago, Leucippus' daughters both
Belong to us. It's you who changed the rules,
Played on his greed with gifts of oxen, mules,
Other such goods, and stole our brides-to-be.
Time after time (though words come hard to me)
I've said my piece, hoping you'd make amends.
What hero's conduct is it, or what friend's,
To come between a bridegroom and his bride?
From Argos or Messene, from the wide
Lowlands of Sparta, from Achaea's towns,
From high Arcadia with its sheep cropped downs,
Horse-breeding Elis or Ephyra's coast,
The flower of girlhood, all our land can boast
Of tact and beauty, waits for you to choose.
The choice once made, what parent will refuse,

Since no one bears a name to equal yours
Nor claims descent from nobler ancestors?
Only give back our brides, leave us in peace,
And we'll soon find you girls well-born as these.
But to no purpose. Patience and good sense
Made no impression. All my arguments
Were blown adrift and scattered on the winds.
Once more I beg you, cousins! Change your minds.'
'If peace is what you want,' Castor replied,
'Renounce your grievance and be satisfied.
But, Lynceus, if your heart is set on war,
Let two join battle here, instead of four.
While Idas and bold Pollux stand aloof,
Our hands shall put this quarrel to the proof.
We'll take first place although we lack their years,
Fighting it out alone with blood-bathed spears.
Our parents will be spared some grief that way.
One death's enough; yet not too much to pay
On either side, if the others are released
To welcome glad friends to a wedding feast.'
Heaven gave his words effect. Both sides agreed.
The firstborn put their weapons down and freed
Their harnessed shoulders. Lynceus took the field,
The great spear quivering forward by his shield.
Then Castor came, his lance poised to strike home.
Above each helmet swayed a horsehair plume.
Quickly they drew together, thrusting in
Their spear-blades where the brown of naked skin
Offered a mark. But the points stuck and broke
In the broad shields before a wounding stroke
Could be delivered. Swords drawn, they fought on,
Each one intent to strike the other down.
Castor hurled blows upon his cousin's shield.
Sharp-eyed for openings, Lynceus barely failed
To hack the crimson plume, and fiercely paid
Back stroke for stroke. Then Castor, seeing the blade
Aimed at his left knee, vaulted back and chopped
The fingers from the hilt. The weapon dropped.
Lynceus ran towards his father's monument
Where Idas watched which way the battle went.
Tyndareus' son gave chase, thrust in the steel,
Pierced him from flank to navel. Down he fell,
Spilling his guts, his body curled in pain;

Death, like a heavy tide, swept through his brain.
Nor would Laocosa see her elder son,
Idas, bring home a bride, fought-for and won.
Tearing a marble pillar from the grave
He made for Castor. But Zeus, quick to save
His murderous offspring, struck the stone aside
Even as he aimed, so that the blow fell wide;
Then hurled a bolt. One flash of lightning, and he died.

★

The man who fights Tyndareus's sons is the loser.
Their power is not to be challenged. It comes from heaven.
Goodbye now, children of Leda, and may you send
My hymns long-lasting fame! All poets are cherished
By Castor and Pollux, by Helen, by the heroes
Who accompanied Menelaus in the sack of Troy.
They owe their glory to a poet, the man of Chios
Who took for theme Priam's city, the Achaean ships,
The battles round Troy, and Achilles, tower of the field.
I, too, offer tokens of the clear-voiced Muses –
As many as they will provide and my house can store:
Poems are the gift which gods are most grateful for.

24 *The Childhood of Heracles*

Heracles was ten months old. The Queen of Midea,
Alcmene, had laid him with Iphicles, his brother,
Younger than him by a night, in the bronze shield
Taken by Amphitryon when he killed Pterelaus.
She had cleaned and suckled them. Now both lay quiet,
Drowsy with milk, as she stroked their heads and whispered,
'Sleep soundly until it's time to stir, my boys,
My own, my innocent ones. Sleep through till dawn
And wake up happy as when you closed your eyes.'
Gently she rocked the cradle, and they fell asleep.
But as the Bear swung westward in the midnight sky,
Leaning on Orion, who turned his giant shoulder,
Hera the artful summoned two monstrous snakes
To eat little Heracles. The steel-blue scales
Stood up as they rippled their coils. Toward the palace,
Past the wide threshold, through the deepset doors
They slid, unwinding their long bellies, flickering
Their tongues, nearer and nearer, greedy for blood;
Their eyes blazing a fiery trail as they came
And their mouths spilling poison. But Zeus was alert
To her scheme. At the last moment, Alcmene's children
Started awake and the palace was filled with light.
No sooner had Iphicles caught sight of the brutes
Than he screamed and kicked away the woollen blanket,
Thrashing his limbs in fright. Heracles faced them,
Shot out both hands and, taking hold of their throats
At the point where snakes distil the venomous juice
Which even gods loathe, locked them tight in his grip.
They wound their tense coils round the nursling boy
(Though still unweaned, he let out never a whimper),
Strained their spines close, then loosened them in anguish,
Struggling to free themselves from his stranglehold.
Alcmene heard the scream, was the first to wake.
'Amphitryon, hurry, get up! There's something wrong.
Hurry! Don't wait to put on your sandals. I'm scared.
Can't you hear the younger boy crying his head off?
Look how the walls are lit up. They show as plainly
As if it were dawn, and yet it's the dead of night.
Some evil thing has come into the house. I feel it!'

Even as she spoke, Amphitryon was on his feet
And stretching to lift his splendid sword from the peg
Where it hung ready above the cedarwood bed.
He had just taken the lotus sheath in one hand
And was reaching out for the newly-woven baldric
When the wide chamber darkened and night came back.
He called to his slaves where they lay lost in sleep,
'Up, my slaves! Bring lights as quick as you can,
Lights from the hearth. Push back the bolts from the doors.'
A Phoenician woman who slept where the corn was ground
Took up the cry, 'Up, slaves! It's the master calling.'
The lamps were kindled. In came the slaves. At once
The house was filled with rushing people.
                                                    The sight
Which met their eyes brought one and all to a standstill:
A baby clutching serpents in his delicate hands.
They gasped their astonishment. Heracles held out
The snakes for his father to see, childishly happy,
And bounced his little body, then laughed and laid them,
Transformed to harmless toys, at Amphitryon's feet.
Alcmene caught up Iphicles in her arms –
The boy was stiff with terror – and held him close,
While Amphitryon settled Heracles under the blanket
And went back to bed to try to get some sleep.

The cocks had barely begun to crow up the dawn
When Alcmene called Teiresias the prophet to her.
She told him what had happened and asked its meaning,
Since he saw into the truth of things without fail.
'If heaven has trouble laid up for us, say it out!
No one can be saved by ignorance when the thread
Unwinds on the fateful bobbin. The insight is yours,
Son of Eueres. I only teach you what you know.'
So spoke the queen. The blind seer gave his answer,
'Grandchild of Perseus, mother of a boy as fine,
Learn courage from them, and listen to the better part
Of what is to be. I swear by these eyes' lost light
That Alcmene's name will live in the songs of spinners
As they sit late, rubbing soft yarn across their knees,
And that you will be honoured among Argive women.
Your little son will grow up a broad-chested hero
And climb to his place in the star-laden skies:
All other beasts and men will be less than he.

Twelve labours finished, and stripped of his mortal parts
By a pyre on Trachis, he will live in Zeus's court,
And, marrying there, will win for parent the goddess
Who sent the serpents to destroy him as a child.
For now, lady, keep fire ready beneath the ashes;
Gather up dry sticks, camelthorn, bramble, briar;
Fetch pearwood, sapless and windbent, from the hillside;
Burn the two snakes on this heap of wild kindling
At dead of night, when they would have killed your boy.
Have one of your maids gather the ashes at dawn;
Send her to scatter them on the rocky wasteground
Beyond the river-border; and see she returns
Without looking back. Purify the house with incense,
Then take a woolbound spray, as the custom is,
And sprinkle salted water about the chambers.
Lastly, kill a boar-pig for Zeus the Master,
To make you master of those who come against you.'
Having spoken, Teiresias rose from his ivory seat
And hurried off, unhindered by his weight of years.

Heracles grew like a young sapling in an orchard,
Tended by his mother and called Amphitryon's child.
He learnt his letters from the old hero, Linus,
Apollo's son, a watchful tutor for a prince.
Eurytus, rich in ancient acres, showed him
How to string a bow and loose a shaft at its mark.
He was taught to shape his hands to the boxwood lyre
And made a singer by Eumolpus, Philammon's son.
As many tricks as the wrestlers of Argos practise
To hurl each other to the ground; the boxer's craft
Of hurting with leather thongs, and all the deceits
Of the fighting-floor by which champions stand or fall,
The boy was taught by Harpalycus of Panopaeus,
The son of Hermes, whom even on a distant view
– Scowling look and brow jutting like a rampart –
No adversary would care to face in the ring.
How to drive a team, how to clear the turning-post
As closely as might be with wheel-hub undamaged,
Were skills which Amphitryon fondly reserved as his own
To teach his son. Often he had brought back trophies
From the games in Argos, land of horses; his chariots
Remained unbroken till their thongs grew slack with age.
To aim at his man, to withstand the stroke of swords

With spear on guard and shoulder covered by shield,
To weigh up the enemy's advancing line,
To order the ranks, to manage a squadron of horse:
All this he learned from Castor, son of Hippalus,
An exile from Argos, where his estate and vineyard
Were held by Tydeus, a gift from Adrastus the king.
Among the demigods, none could equal Castor
As a warrior, until age had blunted his strength.

This was the schooling Alcmene found for her son.
His chosen bed – it made him proud – was a lionskin
Spread on the floor, close to where his father lay.
For supper he ate roast meat and a coarse brown loaf
Which filled a basket – a country labourer's meal.
By day he took little, and that little uncooked.
His simple tunic reached hardly below his knee…

The text breaks off here. The rest of the poem, about thirty lines, is lost.

26   *The Bacchae*

Ino, Autonoa, white-cheeked Agave,
Three sisters, each led out a company
To gather oak-sprays, ivy, daffodils,
And set up twelve green altars in the hills,
Three to Semele, to Dionysus nine.
An open meadow served them for a shrine.

Taking some holy objects from a chest
They set them reverently in place, and dressed
The altars in the god's own secret way.
Pentheus observed the rite from where he lay
Crouched in a mastich bush which grew nearby.
Autonoa saw him, leapt up with a cry
And, kicking out, scattered the mysteries
Not to be known by his profaning eyes.
Sheer madness seized the women, every one.
Pentheus took to his heels. They ran him down,
Hitching their belted skirts above the knee.
He asked in terror, 'What do you want of me?'
Autonoa jeered, 'We'll show you soon enough!'
His mother roared and wrenched his head clean off,
Holding it as a lioness guards her young.
His two aunts grappled with his trunk and wrung
The arms away, treading down on his chest.
His legs, bowels, sides, were shared among the rest.
Thebes saw them come, a blood-bespattered train,
Bringing not Pentheus from the hills but pain.

So let him perish. Righteousness is all.
However sharp the doom, no tears must fall
For the transgressors, grown men or young boys,
Whom the god's hate impartially destroys.
Through righteousness the eagle's place is won.
Good fortune waits on every wise man's son.

Farewell, Dionysus, you whom Zeus on high
Set gently down, the foundling of his thigh,
On snowy Dracanus. Semele, farewell.
And you, her honoured sisters. You did well,
Daughters of Cadmus, to shed impious blood.
Let no man cavil. It was an act of god.

28   *The Distaff*

Distaff, grey-eyed Athene's gift to spinners,
To careful women, proud of their housekeeping,
Come with me to the city Neleus founded
Where reeds grow green in Aphrodite's precinct.
I pray we get a fair wind for the voyage.
There Nicias waits, child of the tuneful Graces,
– How I look forward to my old friend's welcome! –
With him, his wife.
                              To her you shall be given,
An ivory keepsake, intricately fashioned.
You'll help her in her never-finished labour,
Making men's clothes and flowing gowns for women.
If ewes were shorn of their soft wool twice yearly,
Theugenis would keep pace. In all her doings
You'll find her tireless as she's wise and graceful.
Distaff, I'd not allow you to lie idle
In an ill-managed house. You're from my country,
Sicily, and the town which Archias settled
With men of Ephyra, our island's lifeblood.
Now you must lodge in far-away Miletus,
Among the Ionians, in a doctor's household –
A man whose subtle drugs fend off diseases.
There you'll make Theugenis known for her spinning
And turn her thoughts back to her guest the poet.

A small gift to confer so great a favour!
Perhaps. But all that comes from friends is precious.

29   *Drinking Song*

'Truth in our cups', or so the proverb goes,
My boy. Let's drink to that, and I'll disclose
My inmost doubt, to prove the saying true:
I'll never have wholehearted love from you.
Just half my life is mine. The rest I've lost.
One moment I'm a god, the next a ghost,
Sunstruck or sunk in gloom. You want it so
And use your beauty (with what force, I know!)
To take my love and pay me back with pain.
You're young. Though I'm your elder, don't disdain
The advice I offer. Soon you'll learn it's best
To choose one tree for home, and build a nest
Where no wild creeping thing can reach. But now
You range through the whole wood, from bough to bough,
From tree to tree, changing your perch each day;
While any fool with wit enough to say
A flattering word finds himself set above
The 'slight acquaintance' who first taught you love.
No satisfaction? But it's there to find
Where it went missing. Has pride made you blind?
Keep faith with me. You'll hear from all the town
The praise you crave; and Love, who can melt down
An iron heart (mine, for instance), may relent,
Visiting yours with gentler punishment.
I entreat you, by the softness of your mouth,
Not to forget: you can't relive your youth.
Quick as a man can spit, we're past the prime,
Wrinkled and old. As for our early time,
Its wingbeat on the air's a distant sound.
Breathless, we stumble over rising ground
In dull pursuit. Know this and, turning kind,
Take comfort in a love that's undesigned.
Then, though your changed face wears a rough disguise,
We'll still be joined by Achillean ties.
But if you sulk and shrug my words away,
If 'Let me alone' is all you find to say,
(Though I'd fetch golden apples for your sake
Or drag old Cerberus up from Limbo Lake)
Goodbye to my harsh longing! Should we meet
And you call out, I will not cross the street.

30 *The Fever*

I've fallen sick; badly, and there's worse to come.
It's two months now since love's recurring fever
Gripped me. The boy isn't beautiful, but grace
Clothes him from his feet to the smile on his cheek.
The trouble comes back at me, takes hold, lets go.
Sleeping's not easy. Soon there'll be no relief.
Yesterday, as he passed, he shot me a glance
Bashfully sidelong, through lowered eyes, then blushed.
Love clutched my heart more tightly, and I came home
To nurse the new wound cutting into my bowels.
I called my soul in and took myself to task:
'You're up to the old mischief. How will it end?
Haven't you seen the white hair at your temples?
Time to play safe now. Though your looks have faded,
You act as if in the first flush of your spring.
'Crabbed age and youth...' Remember the proverb
And keep aloof from the hurtful love of boys.
A boy's life has the pace of a running fawn.
Tomorrow he'll set sail on a wider sea.
His time of flowering is spent with his own friends,
Quite out of reach. But memory dogs the lover;
Dreams torment him at night; longing eats his bones.
A year's time isn't enough to work the cure.'
I put this list of grievances to my soul.
The answer came, 'A man who hopes to master
The power of love is like an astronomer
Who reckons the stars up, nine by nine by nine.
I'll stretch my neck out humbly and drag the yoke
Since I have no choice. All this, my friend, is willed
By the god whose tricks reduced the minds of Zeus
And Cypris. I'm a leaf that has lived its day.
His lightest breeze catches and whirls me away.'

Notes and Indexes

Notes on the Poems

p. 3 *The Winter's Task* 'the one spoil': I mean the 'hardened hands / And body's mastery' of the preceding lines. The vision and rest, by contrast, are evanescent and have to be laboured for over again.

p. 8 *The Hero* It is the hero who speaks.

p. 16 *The Day* The twelve parts of the poem stand, without a literal equivalence, for the twelve hours of the day. The middle break in each part represents those 'moments of effacement' which accompany the labour and into which it lapses, though I didn't see this until after the poem was written. I use a twelve-syllable line.

p. 22 *A Stag at Sea* Once a deer has taken to the sea, it can't escape because it can always be seen. When it comes back to land, as it eventually must, the Hunt will be waiting for it.

p. 32 *The Forester* 'On either side, equally clandestine': the poacher has turned gamekeeper but remains clandestine because he is acting with the secret consent of the landowner. The culling of the deer is better done by accurate shooting than by hunting. But offence to the Hunt must, for neighbourly reasons, be avoided. The forester is still an outlaw.

p. 48 *At Vigna La Corte* The epigraph, taken from Horace (*Odes* 1.17), refers to the same landscape as that in the poem.

p. 50 *For Pasolini* 'Vecchio ragazzo di Casarsa', ancient child of Casarsa: the phrase, applied to himself, comes from a late poem by Pasolini. Casarsa is a small town in the Friuli region of north Italy where Pasolini spent much of his youth.

p. 54 *Shadowtail* 'black': the russet hair being, by local variation, of so dark a shade that, with the rising sun behind, the effect is as described. The Greek word for squirrel, *skiouros*, is a compound meaning 'shadow-tail'.

p. 57 *Outside* '*Cammina… se non…*': 'You'd better get a move on'.

p. 62   *Torrent*   That is, a stream which dries up, which doesn't run throughout the year (from the Latin *torrere).*

p. 64   *Youth*   'Jove': I was thinking of the Latin poetic usage where 'Jupiter' or 'Jove' can mean sky.

p. 77   *Sabine Portraits*   This sequence, like 'Monte Gennaro Epigrams' and some other poems here, is composed in eleven-syllable pentameters. I have not allowed for elision across words, though a syllable or half-syllable may be elided within a word. By this rule of thumb words such as 'briar' or 'iron' may count as a single syllable, though to the ear they are somewhere between one and two. The epigraph is taken from Horace (*Ep.*1.16), 'There are hills, quite unbroken, were they not cleft by a shady valley', in Fairclough's Loeb version.

p. 79   *Franco*   '*Calmo, lucente*' taken from Sandro Penna's prose piece, 'Un giorno in campagna'.

p. 82   *Giuseppe*   '*cruda senectus*' unripe (i.e. rawly vigorous) old age, of Charon in *Aeneid* 6.

p. 82   *Maurizio*   '*Eh, la pelle è mia*': 'I'm the one who's risking his skin' (so don't *you* make a fuss); '*L'aria è sincera*': 'The air is clear'.

p. 83   *Adamo*   '*vita umbratilis*': a life remaining in (i.e. hidden/ protected by) the shade. The stress in *umbratilis* falls on the second syllable.

p. 87   *A Sequel*   '*Ma non mi riconosci? Sono diventato brutto?*' 'Don't you recognize me? Have I lost my looks?'; *sc* in '*riconosci*' is pronounced *sh*; '*brutto*': ugly.

p. 88   *Angelo Hang-Gliding*   '*Orti*': the enclosed patches of culti- vated ground, part orchard, part kitchen-garden; '*Pian piano si arriva!*': 'Take it gently and you'll get there in the end!'.

p. 91   *La Risecca*   The name of a torrent-bed (from *risecare* 'to dry up again', or else a contraction of *riva secca*, 'dry bank').

p. 93   *Castagneto*   The title means 'chestnut grove' but is also a place-name, one such grove. The *g* in '*Castagneto*' as in '*voglio*', is soft. Horace's villa is 'the poet's ruined house'; Lalage and Tyndaris are girls mentioned by Horace as in his thoughts in this place. The *e* in Lalage is sounded, the *g* hard. 'twin Graces indeed': twins in fact, as well as in kindness and beauty.

p. 95   *Near Civitella*   '*Vuo' scaldar un po'?*': 'Do you want to warm up a bit?'. The place-name exactly fitted this small civility.

p. 95   *Licenza*   One of the various meanings of *licenza* is 'envoi' or 'epilogue'. It is also, and separately, a place-name, derived from 'Digentia', a river mentioned by Horace ('gelidus Digentia rivus', *Ep.*1.18)

p. 105   *Sybarites*   'incuse': the early coins of some Greek cities, including Sybaris, carry on the reverse, concavely, the image which is shown in relief on the obverse.

p. 112   *Five Sketches*   The quoted phrase in sketch 3 is from *Antony and Cleopatra*; the phrases in sketch 4 from Whitney's *A Choice of Emblems* (Emblem 159, the fable of the grasshopper and the ants) and Lovelace's 'The Grasshopper'. (The phrase in sketch 2 is Smollett's, from *Humphry Clinker*, though that has no bearing on the poem.)

p. 114   *A Likeness*   'suspicions amongst thoughts': the opening phrase of Bacon's essay 'Of Suspicion'; 'Promachos': in the forefront of battle; 'Pella': the capital of Macedonia, a world long left behind by the Greeks in India.

p. 115   *Tufan Express*   'Tufan' is cognate with 'typhoon' and means much the same. But this was the slow train.

p. 121   *The Last Caliph*   This is about the sack of Baghdad in 1258 by the Mongols. Sections 1 and 2 refer to an anecdote told of the last Caliph. When a young servant waiting on him in his library had fallen asleep and rolled on to the carpet where he was sitting, he signed to the librarian to wait till he had left the room before waking the boy. In this way the boy was spared fear and confusion at his mistake. Section 3 describes an incident of single combat which preceded the defeat of the Arab army. The fourth section reflects on the destruction which followed. The story is fully told in vol. 2 of E.G. Browne's *Literary History of Persia*. But some time after writing the poem I realized what my hidden subject, at least in part, had been – a terrorist attack at Athens airport in the summer of 1973, in which I had been caught up some weeks before.

p. 127 *Bread and Brotherhood* '*tepe*': Persian for 'mound'; in archaeological parlance, a hillock formed by successive layers of occupation, equivalent of the Arabic *tel*. A disyllable.

p. 129 *The Pillar* 'assured treasure': I had in mind a passage from North's Plutarch, toward the close of *The Life of Caius Marius*, where this phrase occurs; though my poem disobeys the passage's injunction by also looking to the future.

p. 135 *Common Sparrow* Sparrows were sacred to Aphrodite, and 'notorious for wantonness' (D.L. Page, *Sappho and Alcaeus*). According to Sappho, they drew the golden chariot of Aphrodite.

p. 136 *Richard Wilson in Wales* The eighteenth-century landscape painter.

p. 137 *A Photograph* The photograph was by Thomas Eakins.

p. 141 *Three Oxford Poems* 'Ragwort': Oxford Ragwort was brought to the Botanic Gardens in Oxford from the slopes of Etna or Vesuvius in the seventeenth century. From there it spread along the walls and lanes of the city, then further afield (see Geoffrey Grigson, *The Englishman's Flora*). 'Meadows': these are Christ Church Meadows.

p. 145 *Mr Thewes* Constantine: the second city of Algeria. When Algeria gained independence, the Algerian Jews were driven into permanent exile along with the French settlers. 'Blésois': of Blois; '*cou*': neck; '*cul*': buttocks; '*sensible*': sensitive; '*doué*', gifted.

p. 147 *The Thirteenth Book* A thirteenth book was added to the *Aeneid* in the early fifteenth century by one Maffeo Vegio. Virgil's poem ends abruptly, as it were in mid-story, with the killing by Aeneas of his rival Turnus. In Vegio's continuation Aeneas marries Lavinia, founds his city, and after a short interval is taken up to heaven. Vegio's book was sometimes printed with the *Aeneid* in early editions, as if it were the poem's proper conclusion.

p. 149 *Portrait of a Virtuoso* 'virtuoso': 'a student or collector of antiquities, natural curiosities or rarities, etc.; freq., one who carries on such pursuits in a dilettante or trifling manner' (*OED*).

A Note on Translation

A poem is of its own time and place and can't be repeated. A translation is a reading, and bound to be partial; it isn't the poem itself over again and isn't meant to be, though the aspiration to fidelity is no less for that. My translations of Virgil's *Georgics* and Theocritus's *Idylls* were prefaced, on their first appearance in 1982 and 1988, by introductions in which I gave an account of the poems, drawing out what I hoped my versions had conveyed, attempting to make good the shortfall, and giving such information as I could about historical context and the literary conventions within or against which the poems were written. This isn't the place to reprint the introductions. Instead I set out below some basic facts and observations about the poems. But it may be helpful to say something about what led me to undertake the translations, and about my practice of translation.

I discovered the *Georgics* at school, and was astonished by them. In the calm adequacy of their representations, in their sense of the nature of the relation between consciousness and the world, they showed me what poetry could be. The recognition of something I had wanted without knowing I wanted it was instantaneous. In great part because of this discovery I was led on to the experience of work in woods and on farms, on the coast of Exmoor and in central Italy, out of which the poems in the first four parts of this book came to be written. The translation of the *Georgics* imposed itself: I wanted to get as close to the poem as I could, to know that I had read it, and to see (as a record of my reading) what I could make of it in English. From the *Georgics* I went back not to Virgil's *Eclogues* but to the Greek model for the *Eclogues*, the bucolic idylls of Theocritus and, since the work of Theocritus must be known in its variousness, to his other poems. I had heard on an Italian hillside just such sung exchanges as those between his herdsmen (Giovanni and Giuseppe, whom I commemorate in 'Sabine Portraits', were adepts). This, and my curiosity to know what could be made of such exchanges in English, as well as to know Theocritus himself (by the process of necromancy which translation can be, and had been at times when I worked on the *Georgics*) were my starting point.

My method in both versions has been to translate not the words of the original but what the words point me towards, and for that to look to my own experience. Wherever I can, I am transcribing from a memory of my own: an impression or picture in my mind's eye of something seen and known, or a construction of things seen and known. This is one of the ways in which a translator invisibly enters his version. The other way – since a translator is confronted at every point by choices – is in the consistency and character of the choices made. Where there are proper tact and sympathy, the more the version becomes the translator's own, the more it reveals the original. As a result of my method, my translations are sometimes recast to a greater extent than is usual with literal versions – yet that is what they remain. To keep the proportions of the original I have confined myself to the same number of lines – an exception being the first Idyll, where on three occasions I have suppressed a repeated refrain so as not to break a stanza. I would add, since it is often forgotten, that a translation must be fairly judged, first of all, not by comparison with the original, but with other existing versions. That is where the competition lies, and not with Virgil or Theocritus. Every choice means an exclusion, and on these grounds too it is not news (where the work is of any length and given entire) that a translation is not 'as good as' the original.

The Georgics

The word *Georgic* is derived from the Greek *ge*, 'earth', and *ergon*, 'work'. The poem is the production of Virgil's mid- and late-thirties. He began work on it between 38 and 36 BC and read the finished poem to Octavian in 29 BC, when Octavian had just returned from the eastern campaign which followed his defeat of Antony, and was about to celebrate the triumph marking his final victory. The poem was written against a background of civil war, actual or threatened, and a twenty-year succession of rivalries. Looking forward to a prom-ised new dispensation, it asserts and celebrates the lost arts of peace – agriculture the first among them. The hopes and fears of the time, and memories of the recent past, constantly make themselves felt in the poem, by open reference or by implication. Virgil wrote the *Georgics* in Naples ('Parthenope's kind city'). But he was born (in 70 BC) in the north of Italy, near Mantua, in the plain of the Po ('Eridanus'). He was himself the son of a farmer. His homeground and its surroundings – lost to him, and transformed, when confis-cated for distribution to the veterans of Octavian – are recalled by references in the poem and more often, no doubt, in buried reminiscence. The *Georgics* is constructed on a principle of balance and contrast, and works by analogy, its close descriptions being at once realistic and emblematic. Virgil combines elements of a didactic tradition derived from Hesiod's *Works and Days* ('the song of Ascra'), from Hellenistic poets of whom the chief was Aratus, and from his Roman forbear Lucretius, with other elements drawn from epic, lyric, epyllion and prose. Though cast in a didactic form, his poem is without precedent – a new creation.

The Idylls

What is known about Theocritus must be deduced from his poems. He lived in the first half of the third century BC. He was a Sicilian Greek, from the city of Syracuse, but seems to have spent the greater part of his life in the eastern Mediterranean, where the island of Cos (Idyll 7) and, so we infer, the city of Alexandria in Egypt (Idyll 15) were familiar ground to him. On the evidence of Idyll 17 he was patronized for some part of his career by Ptolemy Philadelphus, the Greek king of Egypt. Idyll 16 consists of a plea for patronage to Hiero II of Syracuse (who came to power in 275 BC), proposing him as the champion of the Greeks in Sicily against the Carthaginians. Though the work of Theocritus is of various kinds he is remembered first of all as the inventor of bucolic poetry, from which the European tradition of pastoral derives. What has become familiar or over-familiar to us is new and strange in him. Theocritus draws upon the songs of illiterate herdsmen, upon the learning and refinement of Alexandrian literary practice, and upon a tradition of mime, to produce his own invention – which, given the Alexandrian passion for tracing customs and conventions to their source, turns out also to be an exploration of the origins of poetry. 'Bucolic', derived from the Greek word for cowherd (and then any herdsman), is Theocritus's own term for the songs of his herdsmen and he is the first to use it. 'Idyll' is not his term but that of later commentators. It derives from the Greek *eidos*, 'form', 'shape' or 'kind'. The word was used of poems in a collection, apparently to indicate that work of different kinds had been brought together. Its modern meaning stems from its association with the work of Theocritus. Of the thirty idylls which have come down to us under his name, eight are now generally agreed not to be by him. I have omitted these, though for ease of reference I have kept the customary order and numbering of the idylls (hence the gaps in numbering).

Index of Titles

Index of First Lines